Don't Be Afraid to Call the Baby Ugly

How The Bigger Discussion Got An Industry Talking

Scott A. Vowels PhD

ISBN: 1499328427
ISBN 13: 9781499328424
Library of Congress Control Number: 2014908273
CreateSpace Independent Publishing Platform
North Charleston, South Carolina

Contents

Foreword

It has been over a decade since I first met Scott Vowels, and learned of his vision and dream. I hadn't met many people with any type of innovative, solutions-based vision related to the future of supplier diversity, and I must honestly say that I haven't encountered many since.

Supplier diversity programs encourage the use of under-represented businesses as suppliers of goods and services to corporate and government buying entities. While the list of under-represented categories is extensive, most companies design their supplier diversity programs to include one or more of the following categories: minority-owned, women-owned, veteran-owned, service disabled veteran-owned, historically underutilized business-zone located businesses, small businesses, and lesbian, gay, bisexual and transgender-owned businesses.

As the head of supplier diversity programs at a Fortune 10 multinational corporation over the course of many years, I've had the opportunity to speak to tens of thousands of diverse businesses across the globe. I've had the opportunity to interface with hundreds of supplier diversity leaders from leading companies and, importantly, I was honored to partner with dozens of advocacy organizations that helped to support supplier diversity initiatives. It took me only my first few short months in the role to see that the supplier diversity "industry" was largely driven by an engine of traditions, processes, policies and prevailing norms that were built on a history of decades-old practices that no one dared to challenge. Try as I might to find like-minded leaders interested in engaging in a discourse around challenging the status quo, I was largely unsuccessful...until I met Scott Vowels.

Dr. Vowels has a uniquely blended set of experiences and credentials that have influenced his world view. Armed with graduate degrees in Business and Economics, professional experience in non-profit, government and private sector environments, and a long list of professional certifications – he was, in my view, one of the smartest guys in the room.

I realize now, as I reflect on those early days, that the common ground between Scott and me was based on a couple of primary factors. Clearly, we shared a set of beliefs: first, in the power of an open dialogue to change attitudes, traditional beliefs and business practices; and second, that such a dialogue should be built on the premise that NOTHING IS SACRED. Driven by the conviction that we, as an industry, had spent too much time walking cautiously when it came to challenging conventional ideas regarding supplier diversity, Scott began to ask the tough questions in a series of conversations and panels that came to represent *The BIGGER Discussion.*

Eighteenth century poet Alexander Pope very famously wrote "Some people will never learn anything...because they understand everything too soon." I suspect that meaningful progressive change has been slow to materialize in supplier diversity, because too many of us "understand too soon" - without seeking to learn that new programmatic approaches may be needed to achieve the goals at the core of supplier diversity initiatives.

As this book details, Scott and his colleagues have done a great job of creating the platform for discussions about the proverbial "Elephant in the Room" regarding supplier diversity, economic development, diversity, small business advocacy, and the impact each of these programs have on our economies, communities and organizations.

The BIGGER Discussion begins to lay out a plan to continue to push the envelope to have a meaningful dialogue around socio-economic issues facing historically disenfranchised sectors of the larger community. Don't take it from me, read Scott's book in its entirety – from cover to cover. It is a blueprint for the path forward.

Brian Tippens, J.D.
Author, *FOCUS on the Fundamentals*
Former Professor, University of San Francisco

Acknowledgements

'Thank you' is the best prayer that anyone could say. I say that one a lot.
"Thank you" expresses extreme gratitude, humility and understanding.

Alice Walker

American Author, Playwright and Activist

I've been working on this project off and on since the first history-making *The BIGGER Discussion: The Future of Supplier Diversity* on August 23, 2012, and had not been able to complete it for a variety of reasons. The primary reason being that I could not articulate, in a readable fashion, why *The BIGGER Discussion* was indeed an idea whose time had come; and why an honest, open, candid discussion around Supplier Diversity (and a host of other issues impacting our economy) was needed more today than ever before.

Don't get me wrong. When asked (and often without being asked), I could and did go on for hours talking about what we were, and still are, hoping to accomplish through *The BIGGER Discussion* as an integral part of its parent organization, The Institute for Thought Diversity. In looking back on some of those discussions I had with others, I can honestly see that I was primarily entertaining myself. In my mind, people just were not getting it and I was getting frustrated because they weren't. Was it me or was it them? (Hindsight being what it is, I can now clearly see that it was indeed me, but I could not see it back then).

Out of this sense of frustration, and after consulting with my fellow co-founders of *The BIGGER Discussion*, Phala Mire and Al Williams, I decided that the only thing to do was to write this book so that the world could indeed catch-up. I boldly told Phala and Al that, although I had never actually written a book - I had written several newsletter articles, op-ed pieces, blog entries and a 200+ page dissertation - I should be able to knock this book out in about a month or two.

Over a year later, I had only written about 25 to 30 pages, much of which does not actually appear in the book you hold before you. As I said earlier, I could drone on for hours about *The BIGGER Discussion* conceptually, but when I put those thoughts on paper, it turned out to be complete gibberish. I have two master's degrees and a doctorate; and even now, I cannot come up with the appropriate wording to describe just how bad those first pages (that took more than a year to write), actually were.

Thank You for Believing in Me

This book would not have been possible without the support and inspiration of so many people throughout my life. I am sure I will accidentally leave some out, but as Jesse Jackson said in his 1984 Presidential campaign, if I have offended anyone, please chalk that up to my head and not my heart. Here goes...

I would like to thank: Mary Vowels, Dr. Robert Vowels Sr., Robert Vowels Jr., Cheryl, Robbie and Devin Vowels, the entire NCMSDC Board of Directors, my new family at Apple, Walter Freeman, Maurice Webb, Mel Gravely, Jonathan Sprinkles, Shawn Cooper, Dr. C. Dawn Carter, Richard Huebner, Donald Cravins, Marquis Miller, Reginald Layton, Louis Green, Dr. Sally Saba, Dr. Fred McKinney, Victoria Fulkerson, Jessica Rosman, Gerry Fernandez, Diane Kenney, Linda Kenney Miller, Brian Tippens, Joe & Pat

Goldthreate, Steve Michael, Mary Wangler, Joann Whitley, P.A. Bowler, Sonya Sweeney, Bernice and Mickey McGuire. I would like to say a special thank you to Christine Garcia and Melissa Buss for spending countless hours editing, reviewing and providing constructive criticism.

Lastly, and most importantly, I extend special thanks to Phala K. Mire and Alvin-o "Al" Williams, my co-founders at *The BIGGER Discussion*. I use the term co-founder generously when speaking of myself. In truth, *The BIGGER Discussion* was the brainchild of Phala and Al. They are two of the most passionate, innovative, forward-thinking people I have ever had the privilege of knowing. Thank you both for believing in me, helping me to find my voice, and inviting me on this incredible journey.

Preface

Not Gangnam Style, but We Are Doing OK

As of the writing of this book, over 32,000 people have viewed *The BIGGER Discussion: The Future of Supplier Diversity* on YouTube. Without question, this makes *The BIGGER Discussion* the most viewed program focusing on Supplier Diversity in the history of the industry, and to date, no one else is close.

Compared to PSY's *Gangnam Style* with 1.7 billion views, and Justin Bieber's *Baby* featuring Ludacris with 905 million views, 32,000 may not seem that significant. However, when you realize that the next most watched video focused on Supplier Diversity after *The BIGGER Discussion* is around 900 views (with the majority of them lucky to get 150 views), the fact that *The BIGGER Discussion* was able to garner such numbers becomes all the more amazing.

As founders of *The BIGGER Discussion,* we wanted to challenge the norms that have become commonplace within the Supplier Diversity industry over the last 20 years, to see if they still hold up in today's rapidly changing economy. We were also hoping to get the viewers to revisit some of the tenets they hold sacred as existing best practices. In other words, we wanted the viewers to think.

I don't think PSY did that (challenged the viewers to rethink existing norms) - although I have to admit I did have to focus when learning the *Gangnam Style* dance to ensure I was doing the moves correctly, in order not to be ridiculed by my 14 year-old nephew Robbie and my 11 year-old niece Devin.

Introduction

What You Can Expect From This Book

Tell me and I forget. Teach me and I remember. Involve me and I learn.

Benjamin Franklin

One of the Founding Fathers of the United States

On August 23, 2012, I had the distinct pleasure of moderating the first *The BIGGER Discussion: The Future of Supplier Diversity.* Since then, I have had literally hundreds of people come up to me all across the country to tell me that they watched *The BIGGER Discussion* on YouTube. To date, this event has become the most downloaded video production on Supplier Diversity in YouTube history, with over 32,000 views.

In each of these conversations, the person has thanked me by saying something like, "It is about time someone had a candid, honest and open discussion about Supplier Diversity." Then, as if the person can see my head beginning to swell, this comment is invariably followed by a few observations about what I could have done better and where I should have pushed the envelope more on some of the topics that were covered. However, it is the next part of the conversation that is the most interesting to me.

All of these conversations would inevitably end with the person eagerly asking me a series of rapid-fire questions that go something like this:

"How did *The BIGGER Discussion* come about?"

"How did you come up with the questions you asked the panelists?"

"When is the next *The BIGGER Discussion?*"

"Is there anywhere I can get a copy of the transcript?"

"As moderator, you just sat there and asked the questions. What was your opinion on what was said?"

"Where can I find out more about *The BIGGER Discussion?*"

With this book, I will answer all of these questions and more. In addition, I will provide some of the background behind the questions, my reaction to some of the more colorful comments and, finally, give you a behind the scenes glimpse of what was taking place before, during and after *The BIGGER Discussion*.

If there is one question I have been asked about, as much as my experiences as moderator, it has been how I came up with the title of this book: *Don't be Afraid to Call the Baby Ugly.* As much as I wish I could take full credit for coming up with such a clever book title, I cannot. On August 12, 2013, one of the panelists for *The BIGGER Discussion II,* Jessica Rosman, Supplier Diversity Manager for Caesar's Entertainment, said in her closing remarks, "...we must have the ability to call the baby ugly."

In essence, she was saying, if we are to have an honest, "needle moving" discussion about the good and bad in the Supplier Diversity industry, we need to be able to momentarily suspend political correctness in order to do this.

I laughed out loud when I heard it. That phrase stuck in my head, not only because it was hilarious, but also because it so clearly and concisely summed up what we were trying to accomplish with *The BIGGER Discussion* in the first place. It is neither right, nor remotely politically correct, to call someone's baby ugly. It is also not right, nor politically correct, to talk about what's really happening in the Supplier Diversity Industry: the good, the bad and the ugly. Yet, in the case of Supplier Diversity, if we are to continue to move the industry forward, thereby honoring those who have gone before us and paved the way for the "collective us" to be here, we must not be afraid to call the Supplier Diversity baby "ugly".

Whether she was aware of it or not, when Jessica uttered the phrase, she had not only summed up the essence of what *The BIGGER Discussion* was all about, but also given me the direction or inspiration I needed to finally complete the book you have before you.

We need to have the courage to address the "elephants in the room" that are acknowledged privately, but never discussed publicly. Just as *The BIGGER Discussion* sought to bring the hard conversations about Supplier Diversity into the light, this book is my attempt to give you a glimpse of what went on behind the scenes to bring the YouTube phenomenon to life.

Bringing this book to fruition has truly been a labor of love. I hope you will have as much fun reading it as I had writing it.

The BIGGER Discussion

The Beginning

Chapter 1

It All Starts With a Conversation

A man must know his destiny... if he does not recognize it, then he is lost. By this I mean, once, twice, or at the very most three times, fate will reach out and tap a man on the shoulder... if he has the imagination, he will turn around and fate will point out to him what fork in the road he should take. If he has the guts, he will take it.

General George S. Patton
American General in World War I and II

Recognizing the Moment

I always believed that I would recognize when a life-changing event happened at the moment it was happening. In every movie I have ever seen or book I have ever read, all of the main characters have seemed to know, with almost a sixth sense, when they were in the midst of an extraordinary event. However, that was definitely not the case with me. In fact, it was not until almost a year and a half after the fact, that I realized that a seemingly inconsequential phone call from a couple of my closest friends would result in me serving as moderator for the first *The BIGGER Discussion*. It would change my life forever.

It may sound as if I am exaggerating the impact that serving as moderator on *The BIGGER Discussion* has had on my life; however, I assure you that this is not the case. After all, I had been involved in the Supplier Diversity industry for about 10 years, and almost nobody had asked me to be on a panel discussion - let alone be a featured speaker at a conference or luncheon. Today, I actually turn down paying opportunities to be the keynote speaker at various events, as my schedule has gotten too crowded to accommodate them.

Recently, I even went to rent an apartment and the landlord said he had seen me on YouTube, and thought I was engaging and humorous. To which I quickly responded, "Thank you, that's exactly what I was going for". Unfortunately, I also discovered that my new found 'fame' did not figure into our negotiations, as he did not even consider dropping the price on the apartment; but it was still nice to be recognized. I attribute a large part of this recent uptick in newfound popularity to my role in *The BIGGER Discussion*.

The Birth of The BIGGER Discussion

In April of 2012, an idea was born (yes, my writing has a flair for the dramatic). As is the case with so many other great ideas, the concept of *The BIGGER Discussion: The Future of Supplier Diversity* arose out of a series of conversations I had over a period of time with like-minded individuals. In this particular case, the individuals were Phala Mire, President of the Louisiana Minority Supplier Development Council, and Alvin-o "Al" Williams, Economic Impact Consultant and Director of the Louisiana Minority Business Development Agency (MBDA) Business Center. At the time, I was President of the Northern California Minority Supplier Development Council (NCMSDC). We were friends and colleagues, and we had over 30 years of combined experience in the business of minority supplier development and Supplier Diversity.

For those of you who may not know, Supplier Diversity is a niche area under the larger umbrella of corporate diversity initiatives.

Supplier Diversity is focused on integrating historically under-rutilized diverse businesses into the supply chains of many of America's largest publicly-owned, privately-owned, and foreign-owned companies (with a large United States presence), as well as universities, hospitals, local, state and federal government departments with procurement responsibilities, and other buying institutions.

Although Supplier Diversity is hardly a household term, like all topics related to diversity it generates heated debates among those involved in the industry when the conversation turns to problems in the industry. Also, like all topics related to diversity, many of the most probing conversations and thought provoking discussions about Supplier Diversity occur in private, not to be discussed in public, for fear of being too "controversial" or politically incorrect.

The concept of *The BIGGER Discussion* was to bring these controversial, politically incorrect conversations out of the backroom, hash them out in a public forum, and eventually take them into the boardroom. As the founders, we were willing to take on the challenge of having "real" conversations about the issues and challenges that are obvious to everyone in the industry, but which have been swept under the rug out of fear or distrust within and among the members of the minority business community, and of the major buying and supporting organizations.

The fear I am speaking of relates to being seen as insensitive to, or uncaring about, the plight of others. Simply put, *The BIGGER Discussion* was born out of a collective desire to meet taboo subjects head-on, and have topical thought leaders provide unfiltered, honest commentary and opinions about the Supplier Diversity industry. We hoped that this would serve as the foundation for a meaningful results-oriented conversation.

The BIGGER Discussion was our attempt to deal with the "elephant in the room" - regardless of the subject matter - and, in this particular case, the subject matter would be the Supplier Diversity industry. The idea of *The BIGGER Discussion* was born. The challenge now was to bring it to life.

Chapter 2

The BIGGER Discussion:
The Phenomenon that Almost Wasn't

In every phenomenon, the beginning remains
always the most notable moment.
Thomas Carlyle
Essayist, Satirist, Historian

Make no mistake about it. *The BIGGER Discussion* is a phenomenon in the world of Supplier Diversity. The panel discussion that took place in New Orleans on August 23, 2012 is by far the most watched and downloaded video in the history of the Supplier Diversity industry to date. As of this writing, it was rapidly approaching more than 32,000 views on YouTube and is showing no signs of slowing down. If this doesn't sound like a big deal to you, I can only assume that you are not well versed in the world of Supplier Diversity. Not to worry. I have written this book to acquaint you with the basic elements of this most important issue.

Supplier Diversity is Big Business

By definition, Supplier Diversity is a management process designed to increase procurement opportunities with diverse businesses, and to maximize the volume of goods and services purchased from these businesses. In this case, diverse businesses are defined as those that are 51% owned, managed and operated by minorities, women, veterans, service-disabled veterans and small

disadvantaged businesses. However, correct though this definition may be, it does not do justice to the magnitude and importance of the Supplier Diversity industry today.

Supplier Diversity is a multi-billion dollar industry in the
United States. It is also rapidly gaining traction worldwide (a
topic for a subsequent *The BIGGER Discussion.*) Almost all of
the Fortune 1000 companies, as well as the federal government and most local and state governments, have some sort
of Supplier Diversity initiative. In many cases, these buying
organizations have entire departments dedicated solely to
Supplier Diversity.

In 2006, the National Minority Supplier Development Council
(NMSDC) reported that America's largest corporations purchased more than $100 billion in goods and services from mi-
nority-owned businesses (Whitfield, 2008). According to GAO-
12-873, the Federal Government spent nearly $36 Billion with
minority businesses in 2011 (Shear, 2012). The Small Business
Administration reports that the federal government spent $67
Billion with women-owned businesses alone in 2011 (Adeli,
2012).

These numbers do not take into account small disadvantaged
businesses owned by veterans, disabled veterans, LGBT (Lesbian,
Gay, Bisexual and Transgender) or those located in Hub-Zones
(Historically Underutilized Business Zones). As you can imagine,
adding the contracting dollars spent with these groups would
drive the aggregate total far into the billion dollar stratosphere.
The bottom line is, despite what you may or may not have heard
to the contrary, Supplier Diversity is big business!

The BIGGER Discussion Would Be Different... Because It Had To Be

After much heated debate among ourselves, Al and Phala convinced me that bringing to the forefront the subjects formerly thought of as taboo within the Supplier Diversity industry was indeed an idea whose time had come. Finally, I agreed. But as we looked at each other that day, we all knew that we would have only one chance to do this the right way to get the results we wanted.

Prior to *The BIGGER Discussion,* most panel discussions that focused on Supplier Diversity featured representatives from the corporate, government and minority business communities (businesses and advocacy groups). In most cases, the ensuing dialogue was filled with an endless stream of softball questions that essentially allowed all of the parties to talk about how well they were doing in integrating minority businesses into their respective supply chains.

Please understand, I am not saying that there is anything wrong with this, because many corporations and various divisions of government contracting are doing some very impressive things in the world of Supplier Diversity. Additionally, it is important to understand that being seen as a good corporate citizen is oftentimes one of the driving forces behind why an organization has a Supplier Diversity initiative in the first place. These discussions frequently provide the appropriate forum for the corporate or government entity to let the listening audience know that they have indeed been good corporate citizens, and then tell what they have done to prove it.

Corporate success stories need to be told, and there is a time and a place for that. However in order for this concept to succeed, *The BIGGER Discussion* could not be that time nor that place. *The BIGGER Discussion* at its core was intended to move beyond the warm and fuzzy and tackle the often ugly "elephant in the room" and hopefully, be a catalyst for change.

Open and Honest Dialogue Could be Risky

It is important to remember that the whole idea behind *The BIGGER Discussion* was to address the proverbial "elephant in the room", in such a way that the discussion would live on and continue long after the specific event was over. The other issue we faced was whether or not we could actually get our panelists to be candid. If they failed to do so, the whole philosophy behind what we were trying to do would be at risk, and *The BIGGER Discussion* itself could fall apart before it ever began.

I have served as President of two separate affiliate councils of the National Minority Supplier Development Council. When confronted by someone asking me why I didn't do more to champion the cause of Supplier Diversity - and do it loudly and aggressively - my reply was that I was in no position to police and chastise the ones that funded me, namely the major buying organizations and the minority business community. As a result, I understood the risks that some of our panelists might be taking if they pushed the envelope too far forward. Having this insight allowed me to empathize with the awkward positions our panelists could be put in if this was not handled in the right way. My partners and I knew that each of the panelists potentially had something to lose if *The BIGGER Discussion* got out of hand, one way or another.

For example, in the case of a corporate or government representative, an open and honest conversation about what their various organizations may or may not be doing could turn out to be what is known as a career limiting move. On the flip side, the subsequent restraint would essentially make *The BIGGER Discussion* no different from any other panel discussion focused on Supplier Diversity and minority business development.

On the other hand, the minority business owner is in no better position to speak ill of a potential government or corporate customer. Doing so could malign his/her company's reputation within the close-knit Supplier Diversity industry, resulting in being labeled as "hard to do business with". For a fledgling business, having that label could prove to be the proverbial "kiss of death". Obviously, we could not in good conscience put historically underutilized diverse businesses in that position.

Minority business certifying agencies, advocacy groups and supporting organizations are often funded through corporate sponsorships and/or government grants. As a result, they are in no better position to serve as the "whistle blower" and bring to light some of the real problems that do exist within the world of Supplier Diversity. Finding a panel of individuals who were thought leaders in their respective roles, as well as courageous enough to speak frankly about the subject matter, would prove challenging - to say the least.

Wait! There's More ...

Beginning with Chapter 2, I will introduce extra sections at the end of some chapters in which I provide my unfiltered opinion on some aspect of the subject covered in that chapter, based on my perspective as moderator of *The BIGGER Discussion*. On the surface, these chapter extras may seem a little out of place. That said, I feel that the thoughts expressed in the "X.1" sections are important to the overall story being told. They have only been included when I felt very strongly that there was something extra (and of value) to be added to the topic being discussed. As I noted previously, one of the questions I was so often faced with by those who viewed *The BIGGER Discussion* concerned my thoughts about what was being said, or taking place on stage. These extra sections provided me the opportunity to let you in on what was happening behind the scenes (or, at a minimum, what was going on in my head).

Chapter 2.1

So Many Questions, So Little Time

*You can tell whether a man is clever by his answers. You
can tell whether man is wise by his questions.*

Naguib Mahfouz

1988 Nobel Prize for Literature

As Phala, Al and I continued to drill down and determine exactly
what *The BIGGER Discussion* would look like, we also realized that
the "elephant in the room" - in the case of Supplier Diversity - is
not just one issue in particular, but a multitude of issues covering
topics that are uncomfortable to talk about:

- Are minority suppliers being systematically held back?
- Why is there less funding for Supplier Diversity initiatives
  if the programs are still needed?
- Does having an African American President have any
  impact on the world of Supplier Diversity?
- Are minority business owners their own worst enemies?
- Is there truly a business case for Supplier Diversity?
- Are major buying entities and support organizations
  doing all they can to increase minority participation in
  the supply chain?
- Are corporate and government spend goals real?
- Are there too many groups now included under the his-
  torically disadvantaged banner of Supplier Diversity?

- Are Supplier Diversity programs simply veiled entitlement programs?
- After almost 50 years what do we really have to show in terms of results from all of these Supplier Diversity programs?

and the list goes on....

The scary part is that these are just a few of the questions we came up with by brainstorming for about 15 minutes, and we hadn't even polled the potential panelists, the corporations or the minority business community! There was so much ground to be covered. We truly had to temper our enthusiasm for what could actually be talked about in a meaningful way in 90 minutes or less.

Chapter 3

The Panelists: Who Will Step Up?

Great leaders are almost always great simplifiers, who can cut through argument, debate, and doubt to offer a solution everybody can understand.
General Colin Powell
Former Secretary of State and Retired 4-Star General in the US Army

Many are Called, but Few are Chosen

Al, Phala and I arguably had some of our most heated debates around the selection of panelists. Each of us was respectful of the other's opinion, but the discussions were definitely not for the faint of heart. We instinctively knew that the panel participants could literally make or break *The BIGGER Discussion*, irrespective of how thought-provoking the questions set before them were. In the beginning, we had over 20-25 names; but, as we developed the criteria for what we were looking for in a panelist, the list began to dwindle.

In the end, the criteria turned out to be fairly simple. We asked ourselves the following five questions:

- Is he/she respected and known throughout the Supplier Diversity industry?
- Can he/she articulate their point clearly and succinctly, and be entertaining doing it?

- Can he/she tackle tough issues without alienating our audience?
- Would he/she have the courage of their convictions to be honest?
- If he/she disagreed with someone else on the panel, could they disagree without being disagreeable and still be engaging and entertaining?

Based on these criteria, we finally developed our dream list of potential panelists. Now we just had to make the calls and convince at least five of our choices for panelists to come to New Orleans and be a part of the panel. Much to our collective surprise, getting the prospective panelists to not only commit to participating, but to also buy into what we were trying to accomplish, turned out to be the easiest thing we would do to bring *The BIGGER Discussion* to life.

Great Panel – But is it Diverse Enough?

It is important to note that, while we knew that we had selected an excellent panel of experts who met all of our criteria individually, it was not as diverse as we would have liked. We had reached out to women and distinguished members of both the Latino and Asian business communities, but for one reason or another, none of them could commit to being a part of the initial *BIGGER Discussion.*

Obviously, since the topic was Supplier Diversity, we wanted a diverse panel in terms of gender, race, experience and sexual preference. We really felt that we were filling a void in terms of a candid hard hitting discussion, but would the audience "get it" if the panel didn't "look" diverse enough? Moreover, would we lose credibility if the panel were not symbolic of the melting pot of cultures that make up the business community of entrepreneurs and small businesses in the United States?

Eventually, we determined that the mission of *The BIGGER Discussion*, as well as the messages being delivered, was more important than the medium through which they were delivered. Our goal was to serve as a catalyst for future conversations about the "elephant in the room" topics surrounding Supplier Diversity. If having a somewhat homogenous panel fostered interest in the event, and meaningful discussion after the event, we were okay with that. We felt that we would have done what we set out to do.

The final panel consisted of six men: one white, and four African Americans (five, including me). There was no way I could have been comfortable moderating *The BIGGER Discussion,* and truly feel we were making an impact on the industry, if the panel included only African American men. That may not be a politically correct thing to say, but the purpose of this book is to give you an honest behind-the-scenes look at how *The BIGGER Discussion* evolved. Political correctness in this context would be counterintuitive.

Not All Agreed

If the truth be told, (which is the purpose of this book), we did receive some negative feedback from various blogs and message boards about the lack of diversity on the panel. However, in the end, 95% of the comments were positive; and even the "haters" who complained about the lack of diversity on the panel blogged and tweeted about some of the issues we covered and praised *The BIGGER Discussion* for doing so. Whether the comments were positive or negative, there was a common thread: everyone wanted more. This book is intended to meet that need.

In the end, we decided that we did have diversity of thought in the panelists, if not enough ethnic or gender diversity, and that was the most important thing. In looking back, I would venture to say that 32,000 of you agree, based on the number of views alone.

Chapter 3.1

You Won't Hear Me If You Don't Know Me

*"When you write biographies, whether it's about Ben Franklin
or Einstein, you discover something amazing:
They are human."*
Walter Isaacson
American Writer and Biographer

I thought it would be interesting to the reader to compare the panelists' bios, which essentially represents what I knew about them professionally, along with my unfiltered opinions after interacting with them before, during and after the panel discussion. Here we go...

The Panelist Bios

The late great comedian Bernie Mac, in one of his routines during the *Kings of Comedy* tour when speaking of his sisters' kids said, *"I know 'em, but I don't know 'em"*.

That is exactly how I felt about the panelists. I knew each of them on a professional level (with the exception of Donald Cravins, whom I did not know at all), and had a good feeling about their competency as professionals, or they would not have been selected for the panel. Nevertheless, I could not say with certainty that I knew how they would perform in front of an audience, or how they would interact in the panel dynamic. In other words, 'I know 'em, but I don't *really* know 'em'. Here they are:

RICHARD A. HUEBNER: Bio

Richard is President of the Houston Minority Supplier Development Council (HMSDC), a regional affiliate of the National Minority Supplier Development Council, responsible for Houston, Texas and its surrounding counties.

In 1985, he responded to a blind ad in the Wall Street Journal that provided a perfect match for his proven skills in association management and his passion for economic development. Today, he leads 136 major corporations and more than 1,000 Minority Business Enterprises (MBEs) in a common mission to increase and expand business opportunities and business growth for minorities. Under his direction, the Houston Minority Supplier Development Council has been nationally recognized five times as Council of the Year and as Houston's Greatest Non-Profit Business Organization by the Greater Houston Partnership.

Richard serves on the advisory boards of the U.S. Small Business Administration, Port of Houston Authority, Houston Community College, Unity National Bank, ACCION Texas, Harris County Sherriff's Office, Small Business Today Magazine and the NASA-Johnson Space Center Joint Leadership Team. He is a Ruling Elder at Grand Lakes Presbyterian Church, where he leads the Habitat for Humanity program. He currently serves as Chairman of Leadership Houston, is a graduate and Senior Fellow of the Center for Houston's Future, and is a member of the Board of Directors of the American Leadership Forum.

RICHARD A. HUEBNER: My Take

I have known Dick (as he is affectionately called by all of his friends) since 2004. When you meet him, he insists that you call him "Dick" and not Richard. I am a pretty confident person, but if my name was Richard, I don't know if I could insist you call me "Dick" with a straight face. Yet, no one dares attempt some juvenile word play with his name, whether in his presence or not. Let me emphasize that Dick is of average size and build, so the respect he receives (and deserves) has been earned during a lifetime of being an exemplar of servant leadership, rather than from any sort of physical intimidation. He is known for his calm demeanor, and I have never seen him in the least bit flustered. There is a line in Rudyard Kipling's poem *IF* that describes Huebner to a tee: "if you can keep your head when all about you are losing theirs..."

Call Me Dick...Because I Care

How dedicated is Dick to minority business development? A few years ago, he had a heart attack that required emergency by-pass surgery. Within fewer than a few weeks, he was trying to get back to the office against the wishes of his doctors.

Many people within the Supplier Diversity industry claim to engage in minority business development because they are passionate about it, or it is their calling - and I don't dispute their sincerity in making this claim. However, Dick has been running the HMSDC for more than 30 years. This truly is his life's work, and he has the track record to prove it. The term "icon" has become a cliché, but among the NMSDC Presidents, and within the minority business landscape across the country, most would agree that this term is apropos for Dick Huebner.

LOUIS GREEN: Bio

Louis is the President and Chief Executive Officer of the Michigan Minority Supplier Development Council (MMSDC), one of the nation's premier organizations for increasing business opportunities between major buying organizations and minority-owned businesses. The 1,500-member MMSDC facilitates over $14 billion dollars in annual purchases from minority businesses annually.

Prior to joining MMSDC, Louis served as National Director of Supplier Diversity at NBC Television in New York, and as Supplier Diversity and Social Responsibility Leader at the University of Michigan in Ann Arbor. His public sector experience includes management roles as Chief Deputy Director of the State of Michigan Department of Civil Rights, and work for both Governors Blanchard and Engler. He also served on New York Mayor Michael Bloomberg's Minority Business Advisory Team.

Louis was born and raised in South Central Los Angeles. He has an undergraduate degree from Oberlin College, and a graduate degree from the University of Michigan. He has owned a number of businesses - where he learned as much from those that failed as those that thrived. He is currently President of the NMSDC President's Council, is a member of 100 Black Men of New York, is involved in Real Life 101, and served as Corporate Chair of the Hispanic Chamber of Commerce. He has received numerous awards, including recognition by the Michigan Legislature for Excellence in Diversity and Minority Business, and the first and only ICON Award in the history of NBC Television. Under his leadership, the MMBDC has won the prestigious "Council Of The Year" award twice in the past four years.

LOUIS GREEN: My Take

I liked the spirit of everybody on the panel, and I really liked Louis Green. He grew up in Los Angeles on the wrong side of the tracks that Ice Cube used to rap about when he was a member of N.W.A. and later as a solo artist, not the Ice Cube of today that makes family oriented movies like "Are We There Yet?" I must admit the transition from thug, gangster rapper to a modern day Bill Cosby-type character is one that I have a little trouble grasping, but that is my own personal issue.

Louis has a certain cockiness about him (or "swag" for those of today's generation), which can be a little unsettling or even intimidating when you first meet him. In many ways, his "swag" is understandable, because he has successfully run one of the biggest councils within the NMSDC network for several years, despite the ups and downs of the economy. Louis survived the bankruptcy of General Motors (one of his largest supporters at the time), and the subsequent bailout of the "Big Three." He has been able to find unique ways to keep the MMSDC afloat in tough times. The bottom line is that Louis Green is a born survivor, whose survival instincts continue to serve him very well today.

Louis Green and President Barack Obama?

One of my favorite anecdotes about Louis (and there are several) happened around the time when he served as Chair of all of the NMSDC Presidents. I was serving as Vice Chair, and my fellow co-founder of *The BIGGER Discussion*, Phala Mire, was serving as Secretary. Louis informed me that I would have to run one of the scheduled monthly conference calls for NMSDC Presidents. Out of curiosity, I asked him why he couldn't run it as usual. Very nonchalantly, he responded:

Got another meeting at the White House with Barack.

I literally screamed, out of excitement and envy: You mean President Obama? Wow!

To which Louis lazily replied:

Yeah, what can you do when the President calls you? You got to go.

Louis typically takes things in stride that most of us would marvel at. He has an easy manner about him - but make no mistake - in almost every situation, he emerges as a leader in the room who can articulate his opinions in a manner that leaves no doubt as to where he stands.

MARQUIS D. MILLER: Bio

Marquis earned a Bachelor's Degree in Social and Behavioral Sciences from Ohio State University in 1981. In January 2011, he was named Vice President of Field Operations for the National Minority Supplier Development Council, Inc. (NMSDC), one of the nation's leading corporate membership organizations. He works with the NMSDC President to maximize organizational performance among the Council's affiliates, to help align mission resources and strategies, and to enhance the services provided to NMSDC-certified Asian, Black, Hispanic, and Native American businesses.

Marquis was previously Vice President of Business Development for S.USA Life, a wholly-owned subsidiary of SBLI USA Mutual Life Insurance Company in Chicago. He has also served as Interim Vice President of Institutional Advancement at Chicago State University (CSU), Executive Director of the CSU Foundation, Vice President of External Affairs for the Chicago Urban

League, Vice President of the Corporate Scholars Program of the United Negro College Fund (UNCF) and Vice President of Field Operations for the UNCF's Midwest office in Chicago. He is currently Board Chair of the GRANDFamilies Program of Chicago, and serves on the Board of Trustees for the Museum of Contemporary Art and the Board of Directors of the Trinity Higher Education Corporation.

MARQUIS D. MILLER: My Take

As Vice President of Field Operations, Marquis Miller's assignment is to be a resource to all of the Regional Council Presidents, making sure that the Councils are running smoothly in accordance with the standards of affiliation. That is no easy task. Regional Council Presidents comprise a very eclectic group, complete with unique personalities (that is putting it mildly). Each one thinks that he/she knows how best to run a council. For some reason, the phrase "herding cats" is front and center in my mind when trying to describe Marquis' job. The differences among the councils are many - including culture, industry, demographics, financial stability, size and so much more. In other words, Marquis was thrust head-first into the proverbial line of fire.

What Did He Say?

With all of that on his plate, it is understandable that Marquis has to be a master politician. He has to push the NMSDC National Office agenda, get the Presidents of the Regional Councils to do what is in the best interests of the national network as a whole, and make everyone think it was their idea. Let me be the first to say that Marquis is good at it.

I consider him to be a friend; and I have had many animated, and at times, intense conversations with him concerning

NMSDC's strategic plan or the organization's role within the minority business domain. One particular conversation comes to mind. I remember that Marquis used the term *subliminal bifurcation* or something to that effect - and after he used the term, I really didn't hear a word he said. In my mind, I questioned whether *bifurcation* was even a word, and it turns out it is. I looked it up, got the Latin meaning, and replayed the scenario in which he sprang the term on me many times over in my head. I always came to the same conclusion: Marquis won our argument using the phrase, but I had no idea what he said and I am a little jealous! I still do not fully understand the term; but you can rest assured that I liked the way it sounded even then, and I have used it since in my own arguments with others to get my point across. And like Marquis did with me, I have stumped everybody I used it with, and essentially ended the discussion... in my favor.

REGINALD K. LAYTON: Bio

Reginald is Executive Director of Supplier Diversity and Business Development for Johnson Controls, Incorporated (JCI), where he is responsible for overseeing all diverse purchasing activities company-wide. He has been with the company since 1997. His role is to impact the decision making of the executive leadership team regarding JCI's future direction, strategies, and tactics in Supplier Diversity. He has created and championed policies and processes to track and improve the company's diversity purchasing performance. Some of the programs he has launched include: web-based supplier matching and internal tracking/external reporting systems; department and vendor training programs; advanced purchasing strategies to grow diverse businesses rapidly via joint ventures and divestitures; and lead supplier arrangements and strategic alliances.

Johnson Controls is a member of the Billion Dollar Roundtable, an elite group of corporations that spend more than one billion dollars with minority and women-owned firms. In fact, the company has spent more than $1 billion each year with diverse firms since 2002, and was named Corporation of the Year in 2003 and 2008 by the National Minority Supplier Development Council. Reginald was honored by the Council as Minority Business Enterprise Advocate of the Year in 2003 and Minority Supplier Development Leader of the Year in 2008.

He received his Bachelor's Degree in Management Science in 1986, and a Master's in Economics in 1989 from Case Western Reserve University in Cleveland, Ohio. He serves on the Board of Directors for the National Minority Supplier Development Council (NMSDC), and as Board Chair for the Southwest Minority Business Council (SMSDC). He is also Vice Chair of the Billion Dollar Roundtable, and is a member of the Advisory Board for the Tuck School's Minority Business Executive Program at Dartmouth College.

REGINALD K. LAYTON: My Take

Reggie, as he is known by most, is the Executive Director of Supplier Diversity & Business Development for JCI, and has been for some time. He is rapidly approaching icon status among his corporate peers in the world of Supplier Diversity. To his credit, Reggie has developed metrics and programs within his company that have become the gold standard that many other very good Supplier Diversity programs can only aspire to replicate.

Data Driven

Many of the programs designed to build capacity for the MWSDVBE (Minority/Women/ Small/Disabled Veteran/Business Enterprise) community that have been implemented by the regional councils, were originally designed by Reggie and his team at JCI. NMSDC's Centers of Excellence program is one that comes immediately to mind.

One thing I will say about Reggie is that he rarely seems flustered, and most of the ideas he presents are data-driven. I am an economist by training, operating in the world of Supplier Diversity, so I appreciate the use of metrics and data to support an argument. I do know that, on occasion, I have been known to overwhelm my audience with data and metrics to get a point across that may not stand on its own as well as I would like it to, so I am always a little leery of data overload.

I honestly don't think that this is the case with Reggie; but in general, when the eyes of the audience start to glaze over from the preponderance of data being presented, my "spidey sense" kicks in - and I really focus on what's being said and, more importantly, what is not.

Comfortable in His Own Skin

As a Supplier Diversity professional and as a person, I feel that I still have a long way to go to really know who I am and what I want to be when (and if) I grow up. From what I can see, Reggie Layton knows who he is and where he is going. I think he is very ambitious in a good way, so I don't imagine that being the head of Supplier Diversity for JCI is where he will ultimately end up when his career is over (and this is pure speculation). This is NOT because Johnson Controls is not a great company - it is. But Reggie has the ability to connect with people at all levels, and that quality just makes me think that there are big things in his future. I do not yet know Reggie personally as well as I'd like to, as I think I could learn a lot from him. However, I like what I do know, and I have a tremendous amount of respect for him.

DONALD CRAVINS, Jr: Bio

Don is a native of Southwest Louisiana. He earned a degree in Political Science from Louisiana State University in 1994, and graduated with honors from the Southern University Law Center in 1998. As a law student, Don was a member of the Southern University Law Review, the National Moot Court Board and President of the Student Bar Association. After graduation, he served as the Deputy Campaign Manager for U.S. Senator John Breaux, while studying for the Louisiana bar exam. Since 1998, he has been a practicing attorney.

In 2004, Don was elected to the Louisiana House of Representatives. At that time, he and his father, Louisiana State Senator Don Cravins, Sr., made state history by becoming the first and only father and son to serve in the Louisiana Legislature at the same time. In 2006, Don was elected to the Louisiana Senate for the seat vacated by his father. In 2007, he was reelected to the Senate with over 70 percent of the vote. During his tenure in the Senate, Don served as Chairman of the Senate Insurance Committee and as Vice Chairman of the Senate Retirement Committee. In 2008, he ran for Congress in the 7th Congressional District of Louisiana.

In January 2009, Don accepted a position with the United States Senate Committee on Small Business and Entrepreneurship. As Democratic Staff Director and Chief Counsel, Don oversaw all activities of the Committee, including developing policy and legislation that affects small businesses throughout America, and advising Senator Mary Landrieu and the 19 Senators who sat on the Committee about issues coming before them.

In addition to his duties at the Senate, Don is also an adjunct professor at The George Washington University, where he teaches Prosecution and Litigation in Intellectual Property. In March 2012, Don completed five months of active duty officer basic training with the United States Army. He was sworn in to the Louisiana Army National Guard as a Judge Advocate (JAG), and serves as a First Lieutenant assigned to the 225th Engineer Brigade in Pineville, Louisiana.

DONALD CRAVINS - My Take

I have to confess I was a little leery of Donald Cravins after reading his bio - not because it wasn't impressive, but because it was. His bio was so long that I did not actually read it in its entirety until I decided to write this section of the book.

I literally met Donald Cravins for the first time only five minutes before I took the stage with him for *The BIGGER Discussion*, and he left almost immediately after the panel was over for other obligations. As a result, any impressions I share about him will be based on my limited interaction. In the interest of full disclosure, I admit that I will be offering my opinion without the benefit of complete information...but that has never stopped me before!

Impressive Bio...Better in Person

Let me say that, in my view, *The BIGGER Discussion* officially began when Donald Cravins spoke. I truly did not expect much from the "government guy", as he called himself. I have never been very trusting of politicians or many elected officials for a variety of reasons, a few of which may actually be valid. However, I can confidently say, with no reservations, that having Don in a position of power anywhere in the government brings me a level of comfort. He spoke honestly and openly, and wasn't afraid to let his opinions be known. At the same time, he didn't go so far out there that he would betray his political allegiances. He was knowledgeable, sincere, caring, and legitimately passionate about uplifting his race...the human race. These are not necessarily qualities that I am used to seeing in my politicians, but I am thankful that they are readily apparent in him. It is reassuring to know that there is at least one person in a position of power who understands the need for this country to support MWSDVBE development and inclusion within the procurement process.

Chapter 4

The Moderator, Twitter and Oprah Winfrey...
Oprah Winfrey???

Better to remain silent and be thought of as a fool,
than to speak and remove all doubt.
Abraham Lincoln
16th President of the United States

Who Will Be The Moderator...No! Really?!!

In June 2012, Al, Phala and I had another one of our numerous conference calls focusing on the specifics of *The BIGGER Discussion*. We had decided on the panel, and today we were going to pick the moderator.

The criteria for the moderator were relatively straightforward, as were the criteria for selecting our panelists. We needed someone who could ask the potentially confrontational questions without being confrontational. We needed someone who would push the envelope, but not make the panelists uncomfortable. We knew that once the panelists became uncomfortable with the moderator, or felt like he/she was trying to upstage them or set them up, this would in essence kill the discussion.

After many names were batted around, Phala and Al (who I believe, in retrospect, had had a meeting <u>before</u> the meeting) declared that they had the perfect choice. On the other end of the phone, I was eager to hear their choice; and when I pushed to find out who the moderator was going to be, they said - in unison - as if rehearsed... *YOU!*

Their collective enthusiasm was met with dead silence from my end of the phone. A million reasons why I was "not" the one to moderate this panel ran through my head, and at the exact moment when I was going to recite each and every one of them, Al calmly said the following:

"Scott, I know you have concerns. I would too and that is only natural. However, let me ask you one question: how can we ask others to participate if we can't rely on ourselves to participate? Of the three of us, you are the talker, and you have told me several times your gift was being able to say what others want to say but can't, and being able to say it in a way that it can be received". He paused, and then continued simply by saying, *"The bottom line is, we believe in The BIGGER Discussion, we believe in you, and now we need you to step up."*

I was speechless. Al had me and he was right - I had said those exact words about being able to say potentially controversial things in a way that could be received by the intended audience. I played tennis in college and for a few years afterwards on the pro circuit. After Al had given me the rationale for serving as moderator, despite all my objections (which I never actually got to voice), all I could hear in my head was: *GAME, SET and MATCH!*

Scott, You Will Be Like Oprah

I have told this story many times when people ask me for some, "behind the scenes scoop" on *The BIGGER Discussion,* and each and every time it makes me laugh. With this last re-telling of the story in writing, I will gladly put it to bed. As I said earlier, leading up to *The BIGGER Discussion* we had a series of conference calls to make sure we had a handle on everything that was actually in our control. I am not and have never been a details person; whereas Phala on the other hand is a stickler for details, and Al is somewhere in the middle - neither a stickler for details nor as nonchalant as I am, but no matter what the issue was, he had it covered. Our conversations usually went like this:

<u>Phala</u>: *What about X, that's very important, we need to make sure it is on point.*

<u>Scott:</u> *I don't care, do whatever you want - I'm good.*

<u>Al</u>: *Relax, I've got it covered.*

For example, there was a huge discussion that carried over into several consecutive conference calls concerning not only the questions I would ask, but the manner in which I would receive the questions posted on Twitter, as well as the order in which the questions should be asked. The dialogue went much like this:

<u>Phala</u>: *We have to make sure the questions are relevant to keep the audience engaged, and there has to be some semblance of order.*

<u>Scott:</u> *I don't know anything about Twitter, but it'll be ok...I'm cool.*

<u>Al:</u> *Relax the two of you, I'll screen the questions and text them to Scott's cell phone. I've got it under control.*

On one of our conference calls, Phala spent several minutes telling Al and me why it was so important to have the panel set up the way we did. She emphasized the need to have comfortable chairs for all of the participants, who would have to be in them for two hours and needed to be relaxed and completely at ease in order for the discussion to get intense (seemed like an oxymo-ron at the time, but I went with it). It was equally important that we be on a stage high enough so that those in the back of the room would be able to see all of the panelist's facial expressions.

According to Phala, this would also help the audience to feel as if they were a part of the discussion and connect with the panel-ists. Lastly, as we were trying to do something different, I needed to be seated right next to the panelists and not hidden behind a podium. I must admit that I was not as concerned as Phala and Al about the set-up. As a result, I was taking advantage of the fact that this was a conference call, which meant that they couldn't see me multi-tasking by answering emails and signing some checks.

At last we had finished the call, and Phala and Al seemed pleased with all that we had decided. As I said, they did not have my full attention, but I thought what they did not know would not hurt them (or me for that matter), and I felt I had gotten the gist of the conversation. One last characteristic of the group dynamic is that Al is always the cool one, and Phala literally bubbles over with enthusiasm. This call was no different. Before saying good-bye, Phala cheerfully said:

"Scott, thank you for being so understanding and cooperative. This is going to be great. You are going to be just like Oprah!"

Startled by that statement, I tried desperately to recall the details of the conversation to figure out what I had agreed to that would lead me to be compared to Oprah Winfrey. I questioned: *"Oprah?"*

To which, Phala once again reiterated with her trademark enthusiasm:

"Yes Oprah!"

Sensing my sudden trepidation, Al seized the opportunity to use his sarcastic wit and he chimed in:

"Yeah that's right, you are going to be Oprah 'freakin' Winfrey."

This was followed by laughter and a dial tone. At this particular point I wasn't sure what that meant, but I knew one thing: this would be the last *The BIGGER Discussion* conference call that did not have my full attention.

Chapter 4.1

Moderator – Remember IT'S NOT ABOUT YOU

I am a member of a team, and I rely on the team, I defer to it and sacrifice
for it, because the team, not the individual, is the ultimate champion.

Mia Hamm

Olympic Gold Medalist, Women's Soccer

Now seems an appropriate time to let you know a little something about me that may not be readily apparent upon first glance. I am a research nerd. With that in mind, it should come as no surprise that in preparation for what at the time we were hoping to be my most significant moderating gig to date, I did extensive research to find out what makes a great moderator. After spending hours on the internet and taking bits and pieces from several articles and e-books on the art of being a moderator (before my research, I honestly never considered being a moderator an art), I found an incredibly helpful article by Paul Kedrosky focusing on the ten characteristics of a great moderator, the gist of which I would like to share with you now. I committed them to memory and had them on my laptop during *The BIGGER Discussion.* I should note that the following summary is put in 'Scott speak' but I do think it rings true to the essence of Kedrosky's article:

- Be quiet. Too many moderators think they're actually who everybody came to see. They're not! My job as moderator is to help the conversation happen, and then get the hell out of the way.

- Be loud. My job is to visibly and audibly keep the panelists on track, thereby helping the audience to feel safe and secure. If it seems that no one is in charge, the audience will worry that they will be stuck in this room for the rest of their lives. (This one really hit home for me as I have been in the audience on the receiving end of a seemingly never-ending panel, although I may have phrased this in some other way than "Be loud", but I got the point).
- Be prepared. Know the subject at least as well as most of the panelists. You cannot steer a discussion that you don't understand. (Enough said)
- Be an invisible conductor. As moderator of *The BIGGER Discussion* I understood that I could possibly be conducting a chaotic, yet willful, orchestra. In order for this to work, that's exactly what this needed to be…organized chaos.
- Be able to think about more than two things at once. This was huge for me. As it turned out, I would have Al texting me Twitter feeds and providing me feedback on the pulse of the audience, while Phala was texting me possible directions on how to steer the conversation. At the same time, I was supposed to be paying attention to what the panelists were saying, just in case this triggered my own thoughts about what should happen next.
- Be deferential. Scott A. Vowels is not the star. The panelists are. The audience is. I am just there to keep things moving and make sure the event ends on time.
- Be ruthless. While you're not the star, you need to be the audience's advocate on time, answers, and issues and, for goodness sake, cut off filibusters. (As an aside, nothing kills a party faster than line dancing, and nothing kills a

panel discussion faster than one panelist droning on and on and...)

- Be clear. As a good moderator, my job is to ask short questions and make clear statements.
- Be timely. It was especially important to start on time, but even more importantly to end on time. This proved to be especially challenging, because the audience was really into it, as were the panelists.
- Be fun. This should be a given, but we have all experienced enough of the unsmiling, self-important, and over-serious panel moderators. Again, I tried the keep at the forefront of my mind that moderating *The BIGGER Discussion* is not about me!

Now that I was going to be the moderator, I understood that my job was to be entertaining, but not too entertaining; not to inform (that is the job of the panelists); and, by all means, keep the discussion moving along smoothly. Now that you know what I was trying to accomplish, I would like to get your feedback as to how I did and to how I could improve. I am serious! Please email me at svowels@thebiggerdiscussion.com as I would love to receive your feedback on my role as the moderator.

The BIGGER Discussion

The Event

Chapter 5

The BIGGER Discussion
August 23, 2012 - How Do I Begin?

"The beginning is the most important part of the work."

Plato

Classic Greek Philosopher, Author of The Republic

Who Quotes Paul Mooney to Start Off
The BIGGER Discussion?... Me!

Interestingly enough, a few weeks before I was to be in New Orleans for *The BIGGER Discussion,* I had been watching one of my favorite comedians on TV, Paul Mooney. Although hysterically funny in his own right, Paul Mooney is best known for having been a writer for comedic legends such as Redd Foxx and Richard Pryor. On this evening, Mooney made a comment in his routine that I thought was beyond profound, and I was not alone because it elicited a standing ovation from his audience. I had been looking for my entertaining yet provocative way to open up *The BIGGER Discussion* and Paul Mooney had just given it to me.

This was so important, because one of my mentors - a brilliant speaker and trainer of speakers, Jonathan Sprinkles (yes, that's really his last name) - said that the two most important parts of a speech are the beginning and the end. If you have a great beginning and you "stick the landing" at the end by having a great conclusion, more than likely people will remember the experience of the speech or event and speak well of it. I now felt I had a great beginning.

After being "teed up" perfectly by Phala with a brilliant introduction of me and all of the panelists, all I had to do was swing. Unfortunately, I stuttered, stammered and flubbed the line, and the ooh's and ah's I was desiring to hear from the audience for being so profound did not come. In fact, there wasn't even the slightest chuckle; there was just silence.

When describing the feeling of playing an important point on center court at the U.S. Open in Flushing Meadow, New York, the great Hall of Fame tennis player Andre Agassi once said:

"But here in New York, you don't bestow your silence on just any moment. So when you do, it's daunting. It's a sound and sign of deep respect and high expectations—and it's deafening. I assure you, never in your life will you hear something so loud as 23,000 stone-cold silent New Yorkers."

I would argue that the sound of silence that day from the audience in New Orleans, when I needed to jumpstart what we now sensed would be the most impactful conversation on Supplier Diversity in thirty years, was at that moment no less daunting.

The First Question...C'mon Louis!

OK, so the introduction did not go exactly as I had planned; however, I did have one saving grace. Al, Phala, and I had decided that we would open with arguably our most controversial question. Not only that, but the most controversial question would be answered by Louis Green first, who in my mind would be our most outspoken and thought-provoking panelist. I have known Louis for many years, witnessed him in action and have a deep and profound respect for his insight. With that in mind I steadied myself, now undaunted by my momentary verbal snafu. I regrouped, and once again swung for the fences with the first question directed at Louis Green:

We have our first African American President, a minority in the office. Let's forget the fact that he's African American for a second. He's a minority in the office, so with that being the case, I am wondering if we even really need Supplier Diversity? Mr. Green, you're first.

As I was reciting the question, a slight smile came across my face, as though I didn't know exactly what Louis would say, but I did know it would kick start a great discussion. I must admit that I went a little long in asking the question, but I felt the strong need to redeem myself with the audience by showing them that I was indeed entertaining - and thought- provoking too. To say I was shocked by what happened next would be an understatement. Louis simply said:

"No, we don't need it anymore."

And I yelled (silently in my head) to myself:

"Come on Louis... You are killing me!"

The rant in my head continued:

"I've got another one and a half hours of this? Al and Phala must have known this was going to happen!"

As you can plainly see from my rant, the fact that I thought they 'must have known this was going to happen', or in other words set me up, also shows that I am well versed in the art of conspiracy theory. My rant continued loudly in my head, concluding with:

"That's why neither of them wanted to moderate. I would have been a great panelist!"

Clearly, I have 20/20 hindsight, as evidenced by my comment about what a great panelist I would have been. At that moment in time, I had chosen to overlook the fact that there was not one minute during the concept or planning phase that my name came up as a possible panelist. Now, in all fairness (to me), I do have some strong opinions about this that I will share on the proper stage. It's just that, for this presentation of *The BIGGER Discussion*, being a panelist had never crossed my mind. I should point out that all of this dialogue going through my mind happened over the course of 3 to 4 seconds at most—after all, I had a debate to moderate.

In retrospect, Louis had done exactly as I had hoped he would with his answer. He was both thought-provoking and controversial in his surprisingly short response. Unfortunately, for me as the moderator - expecting him to wax eloquently for a few minutes - his "No" was followed by silence (there was that awkward silence again). He gave no explanation, and sat back in his chair as if to signal me that "No" was indeed his "final answer" and no more need be said. If he had been Chris Rock at the end of his comedy show, he would have thrown down the mic after his answer, because he was indeed done.

I Can Finally Empathize With Richard Nixon

Many people have said that the reason Richard Nixon lost the 1960 presidential election to John F. Kennedy was his poor performance in their series of televised debates. Ironically, it wasn't the content of what Nixon said that hurt him, because many people who only heard the debate via radio actually thought Nixon had won. However, for those watching on television, it was the beads of nervous sweat that formed on his upper lip during his TV close-ups that became so painfully apparent to viewers that they could not concentrate on a word he said. The fact that John F. Kennedy was movie-star handsome, and Nixon was... well... Nixon, likely didn't hurt Kennedy either.

During the awkward moment of silence that followed Louis' answer, I could feel the very same beads of sweat that I imagined Nixon must have felt - not only on my upper lip, but also forming on my already shiny, bald head. I had been entrusted to be the catalyst for the first product coming from *The BIGGER Discussion* franchise; and within only eight minutes I had suffered through both my horrid introduction and Louis' agonizingly short (but ironically thought-provoking) answer. I had not regained my composure, and felt that I was single-handedly killing the vision we had for *The BIGGER Discussion* inaugural debate. (Or had I been set up? I hadn't fully let go of my conspiracy theory yet!)

My Salvation Comes in the Form of a Government Official

Still shaken by Louis' answer, all I could muster at this point was a high-pitched awkward laugh, while simultaneously offering up a prayer that our next panelist would mercifully bail me out. That would be Donald Cravins, whom I did not know personally, and had only met moments before taking the stage. I must admit, I had little expectation that an elected official representing the Federal Government would do anything other than tow the party line, which in my mind would be worse than the answer Louis had given...and then Mr. Cravins spoke:

"Fair enough. Thank you all for allowing me to be here today, and thank the leadership for allowing me to be here. I'm the government guy, and

although I know a lot of the panelists here today are going to talk about business, they're going to talk about Supplier Diversity. "

So far, this was nothing special. In fact, to be honest, Mr. Cravin's voice at this point in my mind was similar to that of Charlie Brown's teacher in the Peanuts cartoon. I knew he was talking, but I couldn't focus - all I heard was "Wahwahwahwahwah." I was reading texts from Al and Phala, referencing my Top 10 speaker notes and trying to figure out how to save this debate, as Cravins continued:

"The reason I wanted to be part of this discussion is because I think, as someone who helps the United States Senate craft legislation - many to deal with the 8A program and other preference programs (the women's program, our vets and disabled programs - I watch what goes on in the Supplier Diversity field because, again, if we don't need Supplier Diversity, do we need preference programs in the federal government?"

I vaguely heard what he said as I tried to focus and thought, "Go ahead Mr. Cravins, kick me while I am down, pour salt in my wounds", as he continued:

"I disagree. I think we do need them. But I am glad we are having this discussion and I think since the election of President Obama I have found that, particularly in minority folks, particularly African Americans, we fall in one of three categories, and because we fall into one of those categories it has made these discussions a necessity. "

At that moment I heard the record scratch on the stereo and the music stopped. Mr. Cravins went on:

"We fall into the category that we've got an African American president and no, now we don't need Supplier Diversity and we don't need preference programs. There's a school of thought that we made some progress

with the election of an African American president, but there's still more to go. And then, there're some folks who think it doesn't mean anything, that we're just in the same boat that we were in 20 years ago. I'm kind of in the second school of thought—it's obviously progress, my kids are seeing something that I never ever, ever thought I was going to get to see, a family that looks like them in the White House. However, ladies and gentlemen, I will tell you I'm glad we're having this discussion because it does make it increasingly hard to justify the need for these programs and, even worse than that, when this presidency is over, I think particularly in the government you're going to also see a rush to get rid of all these programs. You had a president who looked like you for eight years, you guys made strides and gains during those eight years, we've got to take things away from you, when we all know that's not necessarily true.

And so I'm glad we're having this discussion. I do think we need Supplier Diversity, but I can tell you from a government standpoint I think there's still very much a need - at least the testimony we hear at the United States Senate Small Business Committee is that programs like the 8A program, programs that help minorities and African Americans, Hispanic Americans, we still need that. If you look at the wealth gap in this country to this day - African Americans, Hispanic Americans - still our median wealth is here; and other Asian Americans and White Americans, it's up here. I think as long as you have that disparity in wealth and median incomes, you've got to have programs that help us."

Now this next part may have happened, or I could be making it up. A light descended on Mr. Cravins, and he began to grow taller as he spoke. Background music from the movie "Shaft" began to play while he spoke. Yes I know, none of this happened. But for me, ladies and gentlemen, when Donald Cravins had finished, I thought - no I screamed - once again in my head: *The BIGGER Discussion - The Future of Supplier Diversity* has begun!

There was so much to be debated in what Donald Cravins had said, and I wanted and needed to make sure the panelists, as well as the audience, caught all of the nuggets that were in there.

A Small Dose of Your Own Medicine

Just as I prepared to issue my own 3-4 minute soliloquy about what had just been said, I glanced down at my Top 10 moderator list. Staring me in the face at the very top of the list was this statement: 'Be quiet. Too many moderators think they're actually who everybody came to see. You're not!' After reading that, I literally swallowed my soliloquy and simply said, "Marquis?" Marquis was very eloquent, rational and scholarly when he said:

"I would say yes, and I would say yes for two specific reasons. One, I don't know that having the first minority president is necessarily connected to the need to have Supplier Diversity. I do think a focus on minority supplier development is essential for the very same reasons that Mr. Cravins suggested; but I also think that when you think about what's good and proper about diversity and for the number of years that Corporate America focused on being more diverse in their hiring and in their community engagement, just like any good stool you have to have a third leg. And that third leg happens to be diverse suppliers.

It's really no different when you think about all the ways diversity inclusion is a part of the fabric of our country, irrespective of who the president is... and before there was a minority president in the White House there were good, strong diversity programs and I would argue that, on that basis alone, Supplier Diversity should continue to be included."

At this point, I admittedly tuned out a little as Marquis finished and prepared for Reggie Layton and Dick Huebner, when Louis offered me my chance for redemption after being visibly stumped by his first answer by asking to jump back in saying:

"Scott, can I elaborate on my "no" so people can understand where I'm coming from?"

Loudly in my head I screamed:

Not only no, but HELL NO...

... and then I stopped, as I realized this debate was supposed to be family friendly, even in my own thoughts. However, I did get a small measure of revenge when I replied:

"We're going to hear from Reggie and then you. We're going to come back to you because I am dying to know why you said no. Go ahead, Reggie."

In just reading my words, it doesn't sound like I said anything to save a little face from Louis' earlier *'No'* comment. However, if you look back at the video, you will notice the intonation in my voice when I said *I am dying* to hear what you have to say. I know Louis understood the magnitude of what Donald Cravins had said, as did everyone in the audience; and I knew he was smart enough to grasp the gravity of the moment. Despite all of that, he now had to wait his turn as I gave Reggie Layton the floor to say:

"So Scott, I think having an African American president is excellent. It's one of the greatest things I think the United States has ever done. Notwithstanding that, though, Supplier Diversity is needed because of different reasons."

Economic Impact: The New Business Case for Supplier Diversity

If my inner child was screaming with embarrassment before, now he was dancing and singing with delight. A primary focus of the work of *The BIGGER Discussion,* through The Institute for Thought Diversity, revolves around proving that the real business case for Supplier Diversity must have an economic impact component. Al has demonstrated this through his Economic Handprint, while I have used economic impact studies for both the Northern California Minority Supplier Development Council and Louisiana Minority Supplier Development Council to get the point across.

Both methods allow for the business case for Supplier Diversity to center around job creation, income generation and tax revenue for the city, state and country. When the Handprint is combined with the economic impact studies, the resulting empirical evidence validates the positive impact that minority businesses have on the economy.

It was in his next few statements that Reggie opened the door for the economic impact of the minority business community to be added not only to *The BIGGER Discussion,* but also to the larger discussion of the business case for Supplier Diversity and minority business development. Reggie went on to say:

"It's about economically equipping historically underutilized population groups, so even though President Obama is in the White House, that doesn't change the fact that you have disparity in economics with minority groups and with women and with people who are driving market expansions for corporations. And you also have the need because—there's the diversity angle—of innovation, and if you don't have inclusiveness in your supply chain, you risk as a corporation missing opportunities to develop new products, to be able to make inroads in new markets both here in the United States and around the world, so you do yourself a disservice by not having Supplier Diversity. So I appreciate what we have with President Obama, but this isn't about how it looks, this isn't about the cosmetics and the picture looking right, this is about the dollars and cents that are in minority and women decision makers' pockets and in their communities."

With his comments, Reggie Layton had just opened that door for the next level business case for Supplier Diversity - now and in the future – and the offerings from *The BIGGER Discussion* will kick it down for good.

The True Mission of the Supplier Diversity Industry

As excited as I was about Reggie Layton's comments, I was just as excited to have Dick Huebner follow up, because as I said earlier, Dick is a very thoughtful, spiritual man - and like E.F. Hutton - when Dick Huebner speaks, people listen. However, before he spoke, I had to let Reggie know how much I appreciated his comments. At the same time, I had to let Dick know that I needed him to rise to the occasion as he had so many times before, so I said:

"I am so glad I am not following Reggie. Go ahead, Dick."

As if on cue, and completely unfazed, Dick did not let me down, when he said with a knowing smile:

"And I'm sad I am."

With these five words, Dick Huebner accomplished two things that I think were brilliant, but went largely unnoticed. First, he acknowledged my mild attempt at humor. But more importantly, the brevity of his response suggested that it was time for us to get down to business and into the discussion, because these issues are serious. I listened intently as Dick continued:

"I believe that Supplier Diversity is needed more today than it's ever been needed, and for a lot of the reasons Reggie just articulated. It's not so much about race as it is about economics. Supplier Diversity was

established to create viable businesses in minority communities to fuel the growth of those businesses with corporate expenditures so that as they grew they would create jobs, economic self-sufficiency, a broadened tax base for the community, lower tax rates and increased spending for everyone's goods and services. In essence, creating an economic engine in those disadvantaged communities that would then fuel the growth of that community, the city, state and the nation. That's desperately needed today as we try, as a country—as a world—to rebound, to re-grow our economy."

Dick Huebner had hit the nail on the head. Supplier Diversity programs were created in the first place because it was thought that those minority businesses that were getting the opportunities would then turn around and invest those dollars back into the communities from which they came, to better those communities. This has happened, but not to the extent that we would all like to see. Dick drove this point home when he concluded his remarks by saying:

"The fact is that there is a growing gap between the 'haves'—largely white—and the 'have-nots'—almost exclusively people of color. That gap has to be corrected and it has to be done in a free enterprise system. We need to involve people actively; we need to be proactive, if you will, about involving everybody in the free enterprise system. It really isn't working as well as we think it is. Yes, race relations may be on a better keel right now, but that can change if the economics don't also change. So I believe that Supplier Diversity is needed more than any time in the 28 years I have been doing this."

Again, economic impact - this was music to my ears coming from Mr. Huebner. The panel was sensing it and articulating it. Now, going forward, it was the job of *The BIGGER Discussion* to prove it.

Actually, the Answer is More Than 'No'

Now it was time to circle back to Louis Green. I offered him the floor one more time on this subject, but this time I was ready for anything.

"Thank you. So first of all, President Obama - a black president - has nothing to do with Supplier Diversity or Supplier Diversity programs. Second of all, I don't believe in programs—programs are by their nature temporary, finite and aren't in the fabric of something. Thirdly, I think folks really should be on minority business - as opposed to Supplier Diversity - because it is about economics, and it shouldn't even be a minority business program. it should be a majority business program. People of color are just steps away from being the majority of the population of this country; ergo, it's going to drive the engine of this economy.

We have already lost the position of being the first-rated economy in the world. That's down to China, and if we don't want to go down to third or fourth or fifth, the active involvement of people of color who are going to drive, who are going to be the decision-makers in corporations, who are going to be the suppliers to businesses, who are going to be the businesses themselves, needs to be a focus—a very intentional focus—of empowering them to do some things.

So when you say Supplier Diversity program, that to me just weakens something that's very, very important. We don't look at it as strategic, we look at it as something to do—it gets pushed off in PR departments of corporations. People can put an ad and say "We care about businesses" and it looks good and doesn't mean a damn thing. So I have a problem with the whole concept of Supplier Diversity, and especially you had the nerve to link it to President Obama. So my answer is no."

When Louis finished implying that he was offended that I "had the nerve" to link Supplier Diversity with President Obama, I laughed genuinely this time because it was funny, good-natured, and I was ready for anything.

The Boston Red Sox used to put up with the antics of right-handed slugger, Manny Ramirez, because he was such a great hitter and an asset to the team. When he did things that were a little 'out there', the antics would be overlooked and Red Sox fans and management would say, "That is just Manny being Manny."

Likewise, Louis' little jab at the end was just "Louis being Louis." This is exactly why we wanted Louis on the panel. He was willing to be a little cantankerous, while also being entertaining and fun loving. As I said earlier, his original 'No' was exactly what we wanted from him. At the time, I was just a little embarrassed that I was not better prepared for his answer. In hindsight, his comment was perfect, and as I wrote earlier:

Thank goodness for Don Cravins!

Chapter 6

To LGBT or Not to LGBT? THAT is the Question

*We choose forward. We choose inclusion. We choose grow-
ing together. We choose American economic might and mus-
cle, standing strong on the bedrock of the American ideal:
a strong, empowered and ever-growing middle class.*

Senator Cory Booker

Newark, New Jersey

The First Text Cuts the Deepest

I breathed a sigh of relief. I had made it through the first awkward 5-6 minutes of *The BIGGER Discussion,* and the last 10-12
had gone pretty smoothly. Louis and I even had a little good-
natured back and forth with each other, and I was finally feeling
at ease and ready to have a relaxed *BIGGER Discussion* - at least
in terms of my personal stress levels. If you pay close attention to
the video around the sixteen-minute mark, in the midst of Louis
and me jabbing at each other, I feel my cell phone vibrate and I
look down to check it.

At this point, I am thinking about turning the phone off because
I've got my composure back, and its buzzing would just be a dis-
traction. Then I remembered that Phala and Al were going to text
me if any really good questions came in from the Twitter universe.
Honestly, I am half expecting some words of encouragement from

either of them, as I clearly have my game face on and am obviously proving that I was indeed the right choice to serve as moderator. I glance down at down at the phone and the text reads:

You're too soft... losing the audience... can't wait... Ask the LGBT question NOW!

Immediately, this text - cryptic as it may read to you - restarted the conversation in my head that I had successfully squelched earlier, and this new conversation went something like this:

I am losing the audience? You have got to be kidding me! LGBT now?! What happened to me gauging the willingness of the panel to go there?

This was potentially a bomb, if the question surrounding the Lesbian, Bisexual, Gay, Transgender (LGBT) business community and their recent foray into the world of Supplier Diversity was not handled correctly.

And who ends up as collateral damage if this isn't handled correctly?

You guessed it!

YOURS TRULY!

Once again... this conversation in my head, which seemed like it took an eternity, actually only took 1-2 seconds, and I began:

"Alright, so one of the things I find whether it's a minority business, Supplier Diversity..."

After only getting those 15 words out, Louis decides to interrupt and correct me by saying:

"But they aren't interchangeable, Scott."

Louis (I say in my head), ain't nobody got time for that! I'm walking a tightrope up here and I think I am about to fall...Really?!

(Admittedly, in my head I have a flair for the dramatic.)

As opposed to responding and giving Louis' comment the respect it deserved, I simply pretended nothing was said, and proceeded:

"However we want to couch it, I think the pool is getting diluted. I think that there are many more groups being gathered into that pool - and whether it's Corporate America or the government sector or the spend - the goals haven't changed that much, but the pool is becoming increasingly diluted.

See...Um...What I Had Meant to Say Was...

I took a deep breath and was prepared to say:

Supplier Diversity started out in the late 1960's and early 1970's with the issuance of several executive orders from President Nixon mandating that government contractors provide more opportunities to minority- owned businesses. In 1977, Congressman Parren Mitchell wrote an amendment to President Carter's Public Works Bill requiring local governments to "set aside" 10 percent of the contracts for minority businesses. In 1979, President Carter signed Executive Order 12138 requiring federal agencies to support women-owned businesses. In 1982, small businesses that are "socially and economically challenged" were added to the list of businesses deserving assistance from the government. In 1999, President Clinton signed Public Law 106-50, which established procurement assistance for veteran-owned businesses.

Soon after the passage of each of these laws, amendments or executive orders, most of Corporate America (or at least those with an existing Supplier Diversity initiative) followed suit and widened the pool of eligible historically underutilized businesses that would fall under their Supplier Diversity umbrella.

Although there have been no laws setting a precedent within the various federal government contracting departments concerning opportunity for the LGBT business community, today this very same community is (successfully) demanding their "fair" share of the Supplier Diversity pool of business. My question is simple: has a program that started out to help minority businesses in the 1960's, and since then has added another group to the mix every decade, lost its way by adding the LGBT community?

I felt that was well thought out, backed by facts and historical precedent. As opposed to controversially singling out a particular group, namely the LGBT community, this would raise the issue of where Supplier Diversity inclusion would end.

What came out of my mouth was:

"So when we're talking about the future of Supplier Diversity and we're looking at 2050, when we're going to be a majority-minority country, then does it flip all the way around? We're talking about the future of it. This time we'll start down there with Dick."

As I expected, almost immediately my cell phone buzzed with the incoming text simply saying,

Really…!!!???

Time to Move Forward

At this point, all I could do was smile. I couldn't pull the trigger on the LGBT question; it just didn't feel right and a lot of being the panel moderator is based on a gut feeling you get as to where the panelists and the audience want the conversation to go - as well as where the moderator is comfortable taking it. I refocused in time to hear Dick Huebner say:

"Well I'm greatly concerned about the trend that we've seen over a good number of years now, particularly at the government level, to broaden the definition of minority or whatever it's called now—historically underutilized or whatever—to include everyone."

My phone buzzed again and I looked down to read:

Seriously, Twitter is blowing up and every question is about the participation of LGBT-certified businesses in government and corporate Supplier Diversity programs while spend goals remain stagnant... Scott, The BIGGER Discussion Twitterverse wants to hear what the experts have to say about this issue!

My first thought was:

WOW! I can't text that fast. That was a long text and it was typed in only a few seconds.

My second thought was:

Is "Twitterverse" a word?

I know I missed the point of the text, but I did appreciate the speed texting ability. I promised you insight into my thought process, but I never said that all of my thoughts were groundbreaking or extremely profound. I listened, as Mr. Huebner continued:

"So we've been able to make the statement - yes - we're growing in our spend, but are we really achieving the objectives we set out to achieve 40

years ago? I don't think so. We still see African American businesses, as an example, languishing way behind everyone else. But yet we can point to our success in doing business with the women, with all the other disenfranchised groups, and I'm not saying there shouldn't be a focus on including them. If that's justified, certainly we should. But let's not take our eye off the ball and give in to the tendency of being able to make it easier to report progress when true progress, at least on some fronts, is not being made."

Whew! There is so much to be unpackaged and discussed in what Dick said. At this point, I am still concerned about pushing the inclusion issue, but now I am considering asking whether the true goal of the Supplier Diversity movement is actually meeting the original goal of closing the wealth gap between minority communities and majority communities. While all this is running through my head, I suddenly realize that Dick is no longer speaking.

Uh oh! What did he say? What were his last words? Where should I go with this conversation?

So Far, I'm Not So Good at Multi-Tasking

As moderator, my job is to pay attention to the panelists and ask probing questions based on their well thought-out replies. I realize I know lots about this subject, and I could go on for days before I turn it over to Marquis. With cat-like mental quickness, I formulate how I will take what I heard Dick say, add a little to it, and pass the proverbial microphone to Marquis. As I open my mouth to speak, my phone buzzes again and the only thing that comes out of my mouth is:

"Reggie"

The voice in my head has never been louder, as it says:

Reggie? Reggie? Where did that come from? You were not even looking in Reggie Layton's direction. What happened to all of the amazingly insightful things you were about to say?

Thank goodness Reggie is a professional and, as a result, he doesn't miss a beat. I refocus in time to hear Reggie saying:

"On the one hand you have Supplier Diversity, which is a set of processes by which an organization would seek to do business with historically underutilized population groups. So, on the one hand, I'm happy that we're being precise in our terms. You have the public sector, with a set of processes that are really political and legislative that deemed who was historically underutilized. Then you have the corporate sector, where they are doing it for a different set of reasons, and we shouldn't assume that the two sets of communities have the same reasons. One might be political, one might be market-oriented, the other might be supply chain efficiency oriented.

That being said, when you expand the pool of classifications as it's called, I agree with Dick. You have to know what you're trying to do. You have to be precise in your terms. Do you deal with an environment where the decisions are made by women? So be precise, have a Supplier Diversity program that supports women's business enterprises.

Do you have a program where you're trying to diversify the base because you see that minority group members are growing, not only in demographics, but also in wealth? They are better educated now as business owners than they ever were - does that present an advantage to you? Then you design your set of processes, your program, so you go after that particular opportunity.

So my point is, on the one hand I'm glad that we're being precise in our terms. On the other hand I agree with Dick: whatever you do to go after those particular strategies, there should be some reasoning behind it and there should be some gain in what you're doing. So it's not about growing the pool and getting the numbers up; it's about what are you trying to do and are you successful in doing it? And you measure your progress based on what you're trying to do. If you're trying to increase spend, fine. If you're trying to increase the quantity of a particular type of supplier, fine. If you're trying to diversify where they are located, you would have a strategy to move suppliers around, or if it's about growing them internationally.

So I think, in this regard, it's not that you're widening the pool. It's what are you trying to do with these groups that are historically underutilized? That's how we do it."

Focus, Focus, Focus...I'm Back in the Game

At this time, I realize there is no point in beating myself up about a lost opportunity concerning what I should or should not have said. A good moderator knows when to go with the flow and when to intervene. At this point things were going just fine, and with that in mind, I gave Marquis the floor and he responded by saying:

"I don't think anyone would argue that more diversity isn't good and proper. I do think that, as the pie has gotten sliced in multiple ways, the fact that there was a pie baked in the first place to provide opportunity is something that we're steadfastly committed to.

The National Minority Supplier Development Council is going to mark its 40th anniversary this year, and we were chartered to focus on ethnic minorities: Asian, Black, Hispanic and Native American-owned and operated businesses. We truly believe that it's important to recognize the significance of diversity, but we're going to stay focused on our charter because we think that, to Dick and Reggie's point, it's really the economic impact that we're interested in - and ensuring that there are opportunities to develop and then deliver that economic impact so that communities of color can be better at participating in the American economy. "

Is He Talking to Me, About Me?

At this point, I smile for two reasons. First off, it's because Marquis is so smooth. He sneaked in a commercial for NMSDC when I wasn't looking, and he mentioned my favorite topic and what I feel is the missing piece for the business case for Supplier Diversity: economic impact.

The second reason is it's time for Don Cravins to speak, and I am expecting something from him that I can really sink my teeth into, and he begins:

"In the governmental programs, you've seen the same dilution. We've seen the definition of minority change and, as you raised, a lot of that has been political and I'm glad you raised the political question. I am one of two African American committee Chiefs of Staff in the United States Senate, and one of four in the entire Congress. And I will tell you, ladies and gentlemen, I can count on one hand the amount of times that I have been visited by African American folks who said 'Donald, we are here today because we do not want to dilute the definition any further of the 8A program'. I can't count on one hand the number of times I've been visited by other groups.

I'm an African American. I would think African American people would think my door is open. It is political, and I think even with Supplier Diversity, you see things being diluted. We have an obligation - those of us who are African American or those of us who are for or against it - we have an obligation to participate in that process, whether it's political or whether it's economic.

So I do mention to folks that I think we've got to step up - whatever side you're on with these issues - you've got to step up your involvement in the political process as well as in the economic process. Whether you're for dilution, and you think we should include more people in the definition of minority, then that's what you should advocate for; if you do not, we need to hear that too. So part of the confusion we've had is that's what politicians have heard, that's what businesses have heard - it's okay, we've not complained. I think we need to change that."

Mr. Cravins does not let me down. He is right, and I have never ever thought about my personal role and responsibility as Scott Vowels, concerned citizen in furthering the mission of the Supplier Diversity industry. We, meaning the ethnic-minority business community, complain to each other about the dilution (or expansion, depending on your point of view) of the supplier pool of those eligible to benefit from Supplier Diversity programs and initiatives. These are the back room conversations that need to come out of the back room, to be had with those decision makers like Donald Cravins.

It is interesting that all of the other historically underutilized groups (women, small business, veterans and LGBT) have huge lobbying connections. If you put a gun to my head, I couldn't name the lobbying group or lobbyist for the ethnic minority businesses community as a whole. I believe the Hispanic and Asian business communities do have representation, but no one is representing the minority business community as a collective entity. It's time to take a look at the man in the mirror for the answer to this dilemma.

Where Does It Stop?

While I was still pondering the impact of what Donald Cravins had said, I was having a little trouble focusing on what Louis said next:

"This conversation harkens me back to the famous quote from the former NMSDC President Harriet Michel, who says Supplier Diversity is now defined as everybody except straight white men because so many things have been added to that definition. And so I think attention needs to be paid. I'm from the perspective that we need to look at this as a national economic issue in terms of everything that affects our tax base, our military security. How well minority businesses do is not an issue of doing something for people of color, but it's going to be how minority businesses go, so will the country go. And anything else that dilutes from that, I take exception to it - because I want my grandkids not to have to eat cat food - I don't want to eat cat food myself and that's probably my future, but I don't want it for them. So that's number one.

Number two, corporations act in their economic interests and self-interests, and that's what they should do; that's why I own stock, I want them to do well. Reggie lays out some ways they look at it, and JCI is exceptional. But as those pools grow, obviously the focus and the quote/unquote "pie" doesn't grow, and so that's the problem. It's not the definition, but resources matched to that, as you articulated. But that definition takes away where our field of focus should be.

With his statements, Louis has gotten to the heart of the matter and the questions that we, as a business community and a country, must answer. Two that immediately come to mind are:

Who are Supplier Diversity programs designed to help?

If the answer is 'historically underutilized businesses', then the next question is:

How do we define a historically underutilized business going forward?

At this point, there is so much information to digest as Louis and all of the panelists have made some amazing points; but I feel like Donald Cravins has hit me in the head with a sledge-hammer with his comments. I make a note for myself, that what-ever causes I am passionate about going forward, I will no longer complain to those who really can't impact the outcome. Well, at least I will not if I truly want something positive to come out of the complaining. I understand that my inaction related to the causes I feel strongly about is akin to not really caring or apathy. I challenge you to do the same, because as motivational speaker, writer, professor Leo Buscagalia said:

"I have a very strong feeling that the opposite of love is not hate – it's apathy. It's not giving a damn".

And I, for one, am tired of my actions, or lack thereof, saying, "I don't give a damn."

Chapter 6.1

Sometimes We Just Don't Have the Answer

I was born not knowing and have had only a lit-
tle time to change that here and there.
Richard Feynman
Scientist, Teacher, Raconteur and Musician

It's been over a year, and I still ask myself why I didn't pull the trigger on the question of whether the LGBT business community should indeed officially be added to the historically underutilized businesses that fall under the Supplier Diversity umbrella. I understand and empathize with the struggles the LGBT community is going through today. In some ways, they eerily parallel the Civil Rights movement of the 1960's. In fact, I believe that the 1968 riots in Chicago and other major cities, along with Martin Luther King's Poor Peoples Campaign, were among the events that led President Nixon to sign Executive Order 11458 creating the Office of Minority Business Enterprise (OMBE), which today is known as the Minority Business Development Agency (MBDA). These events, particularly the riots in Chicago, also led to the creation of the National Minority Purchasing Council (NMPC), which later became the National Minority Supplier Development Council (NMSDC) of today.

The LGBT community is fighting for their civil rights to get married and serve openly in the armed forces and essentially be who they are, free from the fear of any repercussions. Maurice Webb, one of my colleagues in the Supplier Diversity industry, said that the reason he is so passionate about Supplier Diversity is that he sees it as a way to help move humanity to the next plateau of understanding. To me, that is arguably one of the most eloquently stated and powerful reasons to be passionate about Supplier Diversity. If that is truly one of the goals, then how can you not openly welcome the LGBT community under the Supplier Diversity umbrella?

Is the Problem Spend or Inclusion?

It appears to me that the ambivalence about the cautious approach to the inclusion of the LGBT business community within the other historically recognized underutilized diverse businesses has little or nothing to do with some sort of irrational prejudice against that community. I believe that prejudice, at the root, is unjustified and the direct result of ignorance and fear, or some combination thereof. I imagine that the larger bone of contention for those members of the historically underutilized business communities who may be questioning the inclusion of the LGBT business community within the Supplier Diversity goals of major buying organizations has absolutely nothing to do with views on sexual orientation. The real issue is that we seem to keep adding other historically underutilized diverse businesses to the Supplier Diversity mix to be counted in the major buying organization spend goals with these businesses; but the percentage goals have remained stagnant. In my opinion, this is the real issue. Again, this is a potential topic for a later *BIGGER Discussion.*

For example, if a major buying organization (government department or private entity) determined that they would attempt to spend 10% of their procurement dollars with minority suppliers fifty years ago, by and large this meant African American businesses. As was discussed earlier, when I talked about wanting to introduce the LGBT question, it was first important to acknowledge that the definition of minority business has changed (or evolved), and that is okay. Today, the term 'minority business' includes most ethnicities, women, veterans, disabled veterans, HUB zone and many more. However, in most of the cases that I have seen, the spending goals of the major buying organizations have not changed accordingly. In other words, in the example I led with, the 10% goal for African American-owned businesses fifty years ago is now 10% for ALL historically underutilized diverse (the new definition of minority) businesses.

The biggest issue with the inclusion of the LGBT business community in the Supplier Diversity opportunity pool is that the aforementioned hypothetical 10% goal of the major buying organizations will likely not change, if history holds true.

So Why Not Ask the LGBT Question?

So why not ask the question about the inclusion of the LGBT businesses as a "minority" business? I have asked myself that same question too many times to count and the answer is:

I don't know.

For those of you who know me, you know I have a reputation for saying just about anything at any time, with little or no thought about the possible repercussions. The truth is, I often enjoy pushing the envelope, and watching people squirm in reaction to something I have said that I think needs to be addressed. So why did I not do it this time?

I don't know.

I have had friends come up to me and speculate that I was worried about backlash from the LGBT community, and I can assure you that nothing could be further from the truth. As I stated at the beginning of this book, we were hoping for 300-500 views at most, so if I could have said or done anything at the time that would have generated more interest in *The BIGGER Discussion*, I guarantee I would have done it.

I have had almost a year to think about this, and as you can see from the rest of 6.1, I think there are many important issues that revolve around the inclusion of *ANY* new socio-economically challenged group into the collective Supplier Diversity pool. In the end, I didn't feel that in this setting I would be able to frame the question correctly in order to drive the conversation to the real issue. To me, the real issue is the stagnant spend goals, not who is allowed to or forbidden to participate.

This issue, in and of itself, could be its own *BIGGER Discussion*; and, one year later, I can honestly say in my heart that I don't know the reason I did not acknowledge this elephant in the room. That is my biggest regret, and the issue around which I have received the most criticism as moderator. So much so, that in *The BIGGER Discussion 2*, we made sure to invite Victoria Fulkerson, a representative from the National Gay Lesbian Chamber of Commerce (which is the certifying body for gay and lesbian business communities), to participate. That being said, when asked why - on August 23, 2012 at the inaugural *BIGGER Discussion* - I did not ask what I refer to as the LGBT question, my response is still:

I don't know.

Chapter 7

Really...What Is Wrong with Quotas, Targets and Goals?

Nothing can add more power to your life than concentrating all your energies on a limited set of targets.

Nido Quebin, President

High Point University

As the theme of the first *BIGGER Discussion* evolved, we each had a few topics that we individually fought for more than others to be discussed and debated by the panel. The idea of quotas, targets and goals being a bad thing, when used in the context of minority business contract opportunities or in calculating spend with those minority-owned businesses, was one of mine. Besides my own personal interest in the topic, I also believed it could foster a very interesting discussion.

Time for My Topic

During the panel discussion, I was receiving time checks and audience pulse checks from both Al and Phala. For example, most of the incoming texts looked like this:

43 minutes to go....

You should start thinking about when and if you want to take audience questions....

I must admit that my favorite two texts usually said something like:

Say something entertaining, and Be more provocative....

I often responded to these text messages with:

I'm on it.

However, I can tell you now that I had no idea what to do or say after receiving those texts. All I could do was whatever came naturally, and fortunately for me, most people find what comes out of my mouth to be funny - or at least entertaining.

I did believe that the controversy over quotas, targets and goals was a question that Louis could really sink his teeth into and, hopefully, set the tone I was looking for around the issue; so I chose to start with Mr. Green once again. As I predicted, Louis jumped in with both feet, and responded to the issue of the negative stigma surrounding contracting goals or spend targets for minority businesses by saying to me:

"You answered your own question. It's not an economic initiative."

After Louis' first sentence, I was turning cartwheels inside. I have long questioned whether those in and out of the Supplier Diversity industry (especially out of) really believe that there is an economic imperative serving as the foundation for Supplier Diversity programs. With his first statement, Louis opened this up for debate. He continued:

"Those companies that measure it the same way they measure quality, profit and loss; it's more of an economic issue for them. For others who don't, it's not. It's couched to many in the C-suite as a zero-sum game. If this woman or this minority gets a contract, it's going to take away from

this white male's contract, and that shouldn't be the viewpoint. I think that's part of the problem, because people see [that] if someone gains, I'm going to lose, and the majority of the people in the C-suite are still that straight, white male. You have that dynamic, so people are uncomfortable saying, 'I want to measure how we engage our number of diverse suppliers or how much value they're adding."

And then, just as I was hoping, he handed off the conversation by adding:

"Reggie, you're an exception, but you could probably speak to it better."

I have to give credit where credit is due - Louis Green "got it". He fully understood that the idea of *The BIGGER Discussion* was to foster real discussion among the panelists, with the moderator simply serving as the catalyst, or at most, the person who simply introduced the next topic and then sat back and let the panelists go at it. Taking his cue, Reggie began:

"I want to shift the context. Johnson Controls is very successful in working with diverse suppliers. We are going to end up at $1.8 billion this year. But it's not about goals, targets, quotas—it's actually about projects and dollars.

First of all, what generates the need to have a supplier? A project. It's not about a pie where we're doling out dollars and, oh, I'm done with my dollar pie. It's about we need to have a specific task done, who can do it, are they diverse, will it help us satisfy our customers if we have a diverse supplier? It's a different framework to look at it.

And then, on top of that, are there incumbents with poor performance who refuse to do business JCI's way, who want to give us a cost increase? Why would we stay with an incumbent because of momentum and inertia when you have a whole vast pool of excellent minority- and women-owned companies?

We don't look at it as 'we have to have a goal for this'—we've got to have diverse suppliers who can do these projects to solve our incumbent problem or to solve our not exceeding customer expectation problem. So for us, we use the language 'goals,' 'targets' because we're trying to accomplish something else, solve a problem, and minority suppliers and women-owned companies are a portfolio of folks who can help us do that. So it's a different way of looking at it, I think."

Things were going well. We had a nice flow going for the last 10-15 minutes, and I was starting to view my job akin to that of a boxing referee. By that I mean that the less the referee is seen, and the more he/she actually lets the fighters fight, the better job he/she is doing. With that in mind, I simply gave Dick Huebner a head nod indicating that it was his turn to speak once Reggie had finished.

"Scott, I wouldn't categorically say that corporations don't use those metrics. My experience is the corporations that are really driving progress in minority business development are very metrics-focused. They have goals, strong goals, they are articulated throughout the organization, people are held accountable to it, and they can track their return on investment.

Where we're failing in some organizations and we're losing ground in Supplier Diversity is where the Supplier Diversity professional can't justify their existence on the basis of metrics. The higher I go in a corporation, the more the talk is in numbers. So we have to be able to relate to the pressing priorities and those are largely metrics, and so we have to be able to justify our existence by documenting our successes as related to the corporate goals. And there are plenty of companies here today that I could point to and say are very strong champions, very effective where Supplier Diversity is becoming part of their culture because they are being driven by metrics."

Dick and Reggie were incredibly informative, and every time they spoke I learned something. Marquis was very calculated, politically correct, and represented the NMSDC's point of view most admirably. However, from a pure entertainment and informed point of view, Don Cravins was my MVP, with Louis Green following a close second. I was dying to see if Mr. Cravins would be able to surprise me again, as he began speaking...

"I'm sitting here and I've been listening. Dick, you said something at the onset that I've been trying to stop thinking about. I have been waiting a long time to hear a white guy say that black business economics is what is going to make the black community successful."

I literally screamed internally:

SHUT THE FRONT DOOR!

Mr. Cravins continued:

"And I know you guys are talking about corporate stuff and I don't want to get you off of that, but let me tell you why that's important.

I live in Washington, but I'm a Louisiana boy and I read the Times-Picayune every day—and [Perry] I read the Advocate every day. I'm 40 years old and, since the time I was 19, I've seen African American boys kill each other every day. In this city of New Orleans, we have as bad an epidemic as we've ever had; in the city of Baton Rouge, we've got probably the worst epidemic we've ever had.

And I am now convinced, as a former politician, as someone who used to run for office and thought 'I could save the day,' I am now convinced that the only way we can really raise ourselves out of this is through economics. We've always said that, but Dick, I am now convinced that the only way we can make our communities better is to have thriving African American businesses in those communities hiring people, creating jobs and creating good family models."

Ironically, this is to a word the mission around which NMSDC was originally founded back in 1971; and although the mission is still mentioned, it sometimes gets lost along the way. So I was very glad to hear Don make that point. He continued:

"... and so as we have this great discussion about black businesses and what we should be doing and whether we need diversity or not, I just hope we really, as we leave here and all of you watching in the audience understand, and our brothers and sisters who may be white or from another community understand, that's really what it's all about.

We should be tired of incarcerating people and paying that bill. We should be tired of the amount of money crime costs us. We should be tired of the amount of money terrible education costs us. And all of that will be fixed, the educational system will be fixed, with economics in the African American community. So I have had a hard time getting over that, Dick, and I appreciate you saying that this morning because that's what this is all about."

After Don finished speaking, the audience erupted in respectful applause. Several times while he was speaking, the audience offered scattered, encouraging responses that were more likely to be heard during a sermon on Sunday morning than a Thursday afternoon discussion about Supplier Diversity.

At this point in the discussion, the stars and the moon seemed to be aligning and something magical was happening on that stage. The synergy among the panelists was palpable, and I was truly thrilled to be a part of it.

Chapter 7.1

Meaningful Goals Are the Goal

When it is obvious that the goals cannot be reached,
don't adjust the goals, adjust the action steps.
Confucius
Chinese Teacher, Editor, Politician, and Philosopher

Everyone Else has Targets, Why not the MWSDVBE Community?

Without exception, every successful *Fortune 500* company will set sales targets or quotas, profit goals and cost saving goals. There are thousands of bestselling books about goal setting of all types, be they for businesses or individuals. That is what the self-help genre is all about: setting goals or targets and then figuring out how to achieve those goals. This concept permeates every aspect of our lives from the cradle to the grave, whether we are talking about sports, education, jobs or interpersonal relationships. The concepts of goal setting and achievement literally and figuratively drive every aspect of our lives - and they are not only universally acknowledged, but embraced. Why is it, then, that targets and goals seem to be taboo subjects when speaking about how we can do a better job of engaging the minority business community in a major buying organization's procurement process?

If minority business spend targets or goals are mandated, then they had better be soft, and most certainly there can be no real repercussions if they are not met. Now, before I get tons of emails telling me how wrong I am, let me acknowledge that there are quite a few major corporations that do take the engagement of minority businesses within their corporate supply chains very seriously, and do indeed hold their team members accountable for meeting the stated goals. However, I would argue that they are not the majority, and this happens much less often than you might think.

What Can Be Done to Move Forward?

Those organizations that are doing it right in terms of setting and achieving stated goals are usually following five general rules for effective goal setting. These are in no particular order, and have been borrowed from rules for setting sales targets or quotas; but the principles can and should be applied universally to those major buying organizations trying to better engage their minority suppliers.

Simple goals are usually better goals. If the goal is simple and easy to understand, it will in turn be easier to disseminate throughout the organization. Ease of communication leads to easier implementation, more buy-in, and successful execution.

Data, Data, Data. When all else fails, gathering, processing and interpreting useful data on past success can be very useful in predicting what will work in The Future. If the program is in its infancy stage (or hasn't been tracked and measured adequately), there is no time like the present to start. Most companies are willing to share best practices, so benchmarking can be very helpful.

Know the who, what, where, when and why. Understanding who in your company is responsible for managing the procurement of the different products and services seems like a no-brainer, but you would be surprised how difficult this information can be to come by - especially if the company's supply chain and procurement operations are not centralized. It is critical to understand why you have a Supplier Diversity program. Who are the key players in that process, and why does your company care about Supplier Diversity in the first place? Can you tie Supplier Diversity goals back to sales revenue, customer requirements, or the economic impact on the community in which your company operates? These are just some of the elements of the true business case for Supplier Diversity.

Discomfort is a good thing. Much to the chagrin of my personal trainer, I do not subscribe to the 'no pain, no gain' mantra in either my workouts, or my Supplier Diversity efforts (my trainer is more concerned about me not subscribing to the 'no pain, no gain' philosophy in the gym). However, I am not opposed to a little strategic discomfort, nor should you be. Oftentimes, a little tension during the goal setting/achieving process is a good thing, because it can lead to finding common ground and elimination of roadblocks that might slow your progress. Most issues are resolved through the elimination of some or all of your nemesis' pain. As world-renowned motivational speaker Zig Zigler put it:

"You will get all you want in life if you help enough other people get what they want".

A bad process is better than no process. This is undoubtedly my most controversial assertion, and the one for which I have received the most negative feedback. Partly because I haven't taken the time to really explain what I mean by this. If you start with a process—any process at all—you will at least have some semblance of a foundation upon which to build. Conversely, with no process in place, there is nothing to build on and likely never will be (DiMisa, 2013).

Changed Your Mind?

Peter Drucker said, "that which is measured improves," and in the context of integrating viable minority businesses in the supply chain of major buying organizations, this sentiment definitely applies. You now know where I stand, and I have provided time-tested principles that you can apply to your Supplier Diversity initiative. But are you convinced that targets should no longer carry negative connotations in engaging the diverse suppliers?

Here's the thing. It doesn't matter if I have changed your mind or not. If you are still reading this book at this point, then you have become a part of *The BIGGER Discussion*, where diversity of thought is not only acceptable, it is critical. The very idea behind *The BIGGER Discussion* is that diversity of thought and opinions will eventually lead to solutions that can be implemented for the betterment of the whole industry. At this point, I am simply glad you are still with me and, more importantly, whether you agree or disagree, your point of view is welcome. The last chapter of this book will provide information on how you can be a valuable part of *The BIGGER Discussion*, and will, in turn, really help us to move the needle. Until then, we have a few more intriguing topics to cover.

Chapter 8

MWSDVBE Certification: Strategic Advantage or Hindrance to Growth?

What's in a name? That which we call a rose by
any other name would smell as sweet.

William Shakespeare
English Poet and Playwright

What's the Value in Certification?

Having been in the Supplier Diversity industry for longer than I care to admit, one of the questions that is constantly coming up at the proverbial water cooler concerns the value proposition associated with certification. For those who may not know, certification typically involves the verification that a business is at least 51% owned, managed and operated by a minority or group of minority owners (in this case, the term minority is serving as a catch-all for ethnic minorities, women, veterans, etc.).

The verification process usually involves the collection, review and validation of documentation to support the business owners' claim of ownership and control. Depending on the complexity of the ownership, and the organization doing the certification of the minority business, this can indeed be a long and onerous process - taking anywhere from 30 days to 6 months, depending again on the organization performing the certification.

Just in case the debate about the value or necessity of certification among the large buying organizations isn't enough, the minority business community itself questions whether or not there is a negative stigma inherently associated with minority business certification. In other words, it is not uncommon to encounter minority business owners who are resistant to the MBE designation because the term minority is too often associated with a lack of capacity, or even worse, synonymous with inferiority.

The value proposition associated with certification is one that is constantly being challenged, and those agencies and organizations tasked with performing certification are called on to justify its merits. Far too many diverse business owners incorrectly assume that certification is a golden ticket, after which contracts will magically appear. Absolutely nothing could be further from the truth.

On the other hand, major buying organizations often want the certifying organizations to go beyond verification of ownership and control to provide some sort of capability assessment, thereby removing (or at least reducing) the need for the buying organization to perform its own due diligence. This leaves the certifying organizations in a no-win situation; the buying organizations are unhappy, and the MWSDVBEs are unhappy. Both entities have expectations from the certification process that it was never designed to fulfill.

I'm Wrong...Certification is a Hot Topic

Part of the goal of *The BIGGER Discussion* was to have lively, educational and entertaining debates in which the panelists themselves would literally 'argue' their points of view among themselves, with the moderator serving as referee. Thus far, I was not able to consistently foster this type of interaction - and if I couldn't do it with the topics covered up to this point (topics I thought were a little more controversial) - I definitely had no expectations of this type of exchange occurring with regard to the subject of certification.

At the time of the first *BIGGER Discussion,* I was the President/ CEO of the Northern California Minority Supplier Development Council (NCMSDC), one of the regional councils making up the national network known collectively as the National Minority Supplier Development Council (NMSDC). One of the primary responsibilities of the organization is MBE certification, and even I thought the topic of certification was not all that interesting. So, I was more than pleasantly surprised at the energy coming from the panel surrounding this very topic.

You Heard What He Said...Right?

I don't remember anything particularly provocative about the way I introduced the topic of minority business certification, other than saying that MBEs felt that being certified as an MBE in some cases unfairly stigmatized them. As a result, the process may actually have *limited,* as opposed to *expanding,* their business opportunities. I was expecting most of the panelists to dispute this perception and proceed to tell me why. What I was not expecting was the story that Louis told, and the subsequent discussion that ensued:

"I will say in full disclosure, when I owned my business it wasn't certified. I had a white guy who I named as president who would go to all the sales meetings and would do everything, and I had lots of business for a long time. Chrysler eventually found out I was minority-owned and said 'You need to get certified.' I've been doing business with you for four years and you never knew it. I haven't worked with the Supplier Diversity department. If you pay for it I'll think about doing it - but why should I?

Some people are scared of getting into the box. The flip side is, though there are some great companies, especially some Fortune 1000 companies that are really committed to help because it is part of their mission, to help them (MBEs) to grow. Being candid, I think you need to look at the sector that you're in. In some sectors, it's probably fine; in other sectors, you honestly need to think about having a front person out there to do that. It's unfortunate that's where we are, but businesses look at that right now."

It is sometimes said in jest within the ethnic minority business community that MBEs would be better served with a white person seen as the face of the company. Louis exposed that "inside joke" as a reality, by saying that he personally used that exact strategy, and was very successful.

When someone says something that is more than slightly controversial, and that I think the group I am with might have missed (the audience in this case), I feel it is my self-appointed duty to say:

"You did hear what he just said, right?"

And after hearing Louis, this was no exception. I was wholeheartedly expecting a collective gasp, or at least a mild chuckle from the audience, when Louis told this real-world story. To my surprise, there was nothing, no reaction at all. As a result it was my 'duty' to say:

"You didn't hear it from Louis, but have a front-person out there. I'm just taking notes. And don't worry that this is on YouTube."

When I said it would be on YouTube, attempting to be funny, I had no way of knowing that more than 32,000 people would view

The BIGGER Discussion video after the event - thus giving much more credence to my good-natured warning.

The BIGGER Discussion Among the Panelists

To me, this was another of the many seminal moments on that day, and it came as no shock to me that it involved Donald Cravins and Louis Green. As I said earlier, we painstakingly chose all of the panelists for their knowledge, their opinions, and their willingness to share their opinions; so it wouldn't have surprised us if any of the panelists had gotten into a debate with one another. The surprise to me was that the topic that sparked the first real debate among the panelists was certification - and it began with Donald Cravins following up on Louis Greens' story by saying:

"I think it's important that those folks who don't want that designation don't get the designation. For those folks who do want the designation, it's important for groups like this to continue the education. I don't look at it as give a DBE business; I look at it as award a qualified DBE through a competitive process, a contract. We get certified – it doesn't say once you're certified, you're guaranteed business. You get certified in the 8A program of the SBA Small Business Administration. It doesn't mean you get a contract, it's not a contracting program according to the SBA, it's an economic development program. And so DBEs and all the other acronyms still have an obligation to be a good businessman or a good businesswoman."

Honestly, in looking back at the video, I am not sure that Mr. Cravins had finished his thought when Louis said:

"But Don, the problem is this: When there's a mishap you'll hear 'Damn it, we used an MBE and they screwed up. I'll never use an MBE again!' I've never heard, 'I'll never use a white company again.' But you will

hear repeatedly, 'This minority business messed up on this. We'll never use an MBE again.' Some businesses have to shoulder the burden of everyone."

At that moment, Donald Cravins interjected:

"But you and I have been shouldering burdens for a long time, and we continue shouldering burdens every time I see somebody on TV who looks like me who does something stupid, that I don't have to walk out of the house and they think I'm that guy too. That's just part of our obligation and our burden. So I'm with you, that's where good DBEs do have an extra obligation to do a great job, so even when brothers and sisters don't do a great job you've also pulled them up too."

Now please understand, that at this point it took every ounce of decorum in me not to join in with the crowd in praising what Don Cravins had just said. I, like so many other people of color, and specifically African American males, could relate to what Don was saying.

Among many of my white friends, it is common for me to be asked how the African American community feels about a certain issue, or why a certain African American did or didn't do a certain thing. At that moment, I am their window into the collective African American thought process, so I understood exactly where Don was coming from. I just had never heard it said publicly. Don continued:

"That's just part of life. I don't think you throw the baby out with the bathwater. I don't think you let a company who's done business with a DBE say 'Man we had a bad opportunity, let's just get rid of our DBE program.' We can't do that because the vast majority of DBEs are great, and they go out there every day, they work hard and get a contract because they have a great business."

At that point, all I could do was lean back in my chair and smile when Louis once again mildly challenged Don Cravins on the term 'disadvantaged' in DBE. I would have simply said the government came up with that decision to use that designation, not me. However, I did agree with Mr. Cravins' response that the DBEs are called that because they are at a disadvantage. At this point Louis clarified what he meant in challenging the term disadvantaged by saying:

"They're not disadvantaged. They're economically screwed over, but they aren't disadvantaged. They're more capable than more than half of the people out here. So my problem again is with the language".

In the end, when Donald Cravins said:

"I understand. I'm with you,"

it was apparent that they were actually on the same side, and were simply arguing semantics. From a spectator point of view, I loved the interaction. Nothing exemplified more what we were trying to accomplish with *The BIGGER Discussion* than this particular exchange of ideas and opinions.

And Yet There is More

Dick Huebner has been a successful leader in the minority business development arena for more than 25 years, and I knew we would have missed a golden opportunity had he not been able to weigh in on the issue of certification. With that in mind, I was eager to hear from Mr. Huebner and was fascinated to hear him say:

"What does certification mean? Does it mean you're just a minority business - minority owned, managed and controlled? Or does it mean that

you're really in a position to be able to do business with major companies, that you've been through some training, some vetting if you will. Do we have the data? So our role as an organization I think changes from just going out and identifying them, to really preparing them to be successful in this market, and that's challenging.

It also says that we could be collaborative, we can work with a whole lot of organizations that share our mission, maybe at different levels with a different focus, and I think the key to that is let's not try to be all things to all people. Let's get focused on the problem, divvy up responsibilities and let's get the problem resolved.

Our Board has recently said that the Council has become very effective in positioning minority firms so they can effectively compete for, win, and perform on contracts with major corporations.

They said 'But we aren't satisfied.' We want the Council to position minority firms in such a manner that business is attracted to them because they're that good and because you said so. Changing role. So we listen to our customers and say, 'How do we take it to the next level?' We have a whole lot of organizations that are competing with us, they see what success we've had and they say 'I want to do it too, I want to cash in on this.' And my feeling is, we don't need to compete. You do it. Now that you know how to do that, let us raise our level of support and leadership to another level that we're now prepared to do what they're not quite prepared to do yet. So go ahead, there's plenty of work for all of us to do in Supplier Diversity. Let's divvy up the responsibilities and get the job done."

So. Now we had heard the government perspective, and that of two NMSDC Regional Council Presidents on the role of certification; but we needed to hear the corporate perspective, and it was time for Reggie to speak. He eagerly weighed in, saying:

"I think about the question that you're asking and I hear it a lot from diverse suppliers, 'Why do you have to have me in this classification?' And my response is, if you're a diverse supplier you can't have it both ways. On the one hand, you want me to be able to answer the question, 'Well how much do you do with diverse businesses? Where are they located? How have you helped communities of color and women grow?' You want me to be able to answer those questions, but you don't want me to be able to see who those people are. You want me to be not credible.

Do you understand, as we said previously on the panel, that the higher you go up in an organization the more metric-driven it is, so you want me to not have a metric on our performance with diverse suppliers and the impact and outcomes we've had. Is that what you want? 'Well it just costs me money, I don't want to do it.'

Okay, do you want me to promote your business throughout Johnson Controls? Do you want me to promote somebody who looks like they're diverse and we all discover, like the Cincinnati public school example, that the folks they thought were diverse suppliers weren't? You can't have it both ways. If you're afraid to be stigmatized by this designation, then don't sign up for it. You can play your cards the way you see best. But if you want us to help you grow your business, it comes with the territory. That's what I want to say."

Marquis Miller rebutted briefly, clarifying that he did not mean to say 'give' an MBE an opportunity:

"In the interest of maintaining our focus on precise language, what I meant by 'give opportunity' is really to give chances to those firms that have demonstrated their capabilities and capacity - not give them contracts for the sake of just giving them - because it's not something that they're owed, it's something they work at, and the certification process validates that they've worked at it such that they can now participate in the supply chain."

The best part of what was happening now was that all of the panelists were interacting on their own, without any prompting from me. I did not ask Marquis to clarify his previous statements about the use of the word *'give'* - he did it on his own. After Marquis, Donald Cravins jumped back in, saying:

"Maybe we're talking about two different types of minority businesses too. You make a good point. If a brother or sister has a successful business, why should they be lumped in as a socially disadvantaged business for a certain program? I don't think we should get rid of the disadvantaged business because they are people of color who are still very much disadvantaged and deserve a play in that role.

But maybe there needs to be the creation of a new program. I've been trying to float this idea, particularly among African American, Hispanic and some other minority communities. We've got a lot of successful minority-owned businesses in this room, and I'm speaking from the government standpoint… that if you mentor or do business with an SDB, you may no longer be socially disadvantaged. You may have graduated out of the 8A program because you're successful now, you're not socially disadvantaged anymore.

Why couldn't we create a program where there would be some incentive for you now to mentor the socially disadvantaged? You're no longer an SDB, you may be just a minority business owner, but maybe we shouldn't lump people into just one fit classification because it worked when we created the program in the 1960s or 1970s. I don't think we get rid of the original intent, because we still have the same problems and maybe we need to expand opportunity for small businesses."

At this point, all of the conversations in my head are positive for the first time. I was elated by the way *The BIGGER Discussion* was going, as Reggie jumped back in reacting to Don's statements:

"So we're being precise in our terms. This is one of the major differences between the public sector and the private sector. The political sector, of course, has political undertones; in the private sector, you can have a huge minority business and, to Louis' point, there still might be the stigma associated with them being a minority business enterprise. I mean, World Wide Technology, they're $4 billion dollars."

To his credit, Louis was steadfast in his opinion that even billion dollar MBEs may have the negative 'minority' stigma, which he pointed out to Mr. Layton, who responded:

"Yeah. Bridgewater Interiors, Software House International—these are all billion dollar companies with thousands and thousands of employees and they're not small, they're not disadvantaged, but they are minority. So, we need to be precise in our terms, design our programs accordingly and yes, we can have those programs, particularly in the private sector where they're designed to address a specific issue: diversify the supply chain, go after market opportunities or whatever."

Chapter 8.1

What's Wrong with Being a Certified Minority Business?

If you see a blatant error or misconception about your-
self, you really want to set it straight.
Jimmy Wales
Wikipedia Co-founder

Where Does the Negative Stigma Come From?

For small business owners, is being labeled as an MWSDVBE some sort of shorthand for subpar or inferior service? The answer to this depends on the point of view of the person answering the question.

Outside the world of Supplier Diversity, government-mandated goals for the inclusion of diverse suppliers in their at-large purchases are often seen as handouts or, at best, unfair and unwarranted advantages for diverse businesses. I would argue that this view is in part the result of a lack of requisite historical knowledge needed to understand why programs such as this are necessary, but I think there is more to it than that.

The economic downturns of the last few years that have affected all businesses make it harder for non-diverse businesses that are not eligible to participate in these programs to accept the existence of Supplier Diversity programs. In the most extreme cases, a Supplier Diversity program can be seen as unfairly tipping the scales for businesses that otherwise wouldn't be qualified for the work they receive.

Again, the underlying perception of the *inferior* minority business being unfairly 'given' the work simply because they are minority owned to reach some quota rears its ugly head. Taking into consideration the difficult times facing the small business community as a whole, I can understand how any 'perceived' advantage provided solely to the diverse businesses could cause even more tension.

Contract opportunities can often appear to be a zero-sum game, meaning there are winners and losers. If one business wins a contract, in essence the other competing business has lost that contract. The ultimate decision may have been based on quality, price, service, delivery, reputation or any number of other factors. Likeability cannot be overlooked. I have often said, and I wholeheartedly believe, that people do business with people they know and people they like. That is a quality that likely will not show up on a score sheet, but must not be overlooked.

However if the business that lost out to another business is looking for someone to "blame", then it is easier to blame not getting the opportunity on an 'unfair' advantage afforded the company winning the business, as opposed to looking in the mirror to possibly discover the real reason the opportunity was lost.

Why Aren't More MWBEs Certified?

According to the Minority Business Development Agency (MBDA), there are 5.8 million minority-owned businesses generating $1.1 trillion in revenues in the United States. At the same time, The 2013 State of Women-Owned Businesses Report says that there are 8.6 million women-owned businesses generating $1.3 trillion in revenue. On the surface, these numbers seem to suggest that overall minority and women-owned businesses are successful, and not doing too badly as a collective group.

The National Minority Supplier Development Council (NMSDC) and the Women's Business Enterprise National Councils (WBENC) are unquestionably the premiere third- party certifying organizations for ethnic minority-owned and women-owned businesses. Combined, they account for about 25,000 certified minority and women business enterprises.

I will allow that there may be some businesses that are counted by the Minority Business Development Agency that are also women-owned businesses. As a result, I will very conservatively only take into account the reported number of women-owned businesses for purposes of this discussion. That leaves us with 8.6 million businesses. Let's assume that, of that number, there are only 1 million that would provide products and services requisite to being categorized as a "supplier" and not just a business.

Business vs. Supplier

Before going any further, I want to clarify the difference between a business and a supplier in this context. Suppliers are a specific sub-set of businesses. In other words, all suppliers are businesses; but the converse is not true, as all businesses are not suppliers. A supplier is commonly defined as:

A person or company that provides goods and/or services to other companies as one of the contributors to the development process on the way to the ultimate customer. A supplier could produce and deliver raw materials, partially assembled components, custom parts, or any consumable supplies. A supplier could also provide labor, consulting or management services.

A business on the other hand is simply, but broadly, defined as:

A commercial enterprise (which, again, would include all suppliers).

The primary distinction between a business and a supplier in this case would be that a supplier is included as an integral part of the corporations supply chain, involved in some aspect of bringing the product to the end consumer. Examples of suppliers may include general contractors, raw material providers, commercial printers, value added resellers, engineering services, temporary staffing and so on.

In this context, a business that is not a supplier would not be a part of the major buying organization's supply chain. Examples of businesses that are not suppliers would be fast food chains, most restaurants, beauty/barber shops, nail salons, drugstores, mom & pop grocery stores, etc.

As can be seen in these examples, there are no hard and fast rules in black and white for distinguishing between a business and a supplier, as there is plenty of room for overlap; it's all shades of gray. The biggest difference is the intended customer. In this scenario, businesses will likely be smaller, have a local presence and target the end consumer as their ultimate customer. Suppliers will tend to be larger, have a greater geographic footprint, and target corporations and government entities as their ultimate customer.

So, Why Aren't More MWBEs Certified?

Now, let's pick up where we left off in the previous paragraph in our discussion about certification, before I provided the distinction between a business and a supplier. Given these very conservative assumptions that only 1 million of the 8.6 million businesses in the United States would fall into the category of suppliers, it appears that of the 1 million suppliers eligible for certification by the country's two premier third party certifying organizations (WBENC and NMSDC), only 25,000 or 2.5% of the suppliers have chosen to pursue certification.

This discrepancy seems to suggest that the negative stigma perceived by some members of the MWBE community may not be with being known as an MWBE, but rather being certified as an MWBE. If this is indeed the case, the larger question has to be:

Why?

I have been told by many successful owners of minority and women-owned business enterprises that, once it is discovered that their company is minority-owned, major buying organizations will place a ceiling on the amount of business they might receive. If this is true, then certification as a minority or women-owned business could very rightly be seen as an unnecessary burden placed on the MWBE. It scares me to think that this could actually be the case; but if it is, then I again ask:

Why?

The question of the necessity for, and the value proposition behind, minority business certification was the most hotly debated topic in *The BIGGER Discussion.* This is a little baffling, because all third party organizations offering certification clearly list on their websites what their value proposition is - and, for the most part, they are similar, regardless of the certifying body. For example, for the Northern California Minority Supplier Development Council (the organization of which I am the former President), the website lists the following for the value to the MBE of getting certified:

- Nationally-recognized MBE Certification
- Exposure to business opportunities - more than 2/3 of certified MBEs confirm an increase in revenue by partnering with Corporate Members
- Local, regional, and national business referrals
- Listings in the NCMSDC local and National MSDC supplier databases, accessible by Corporate Buyers nationwide
- Participation in technical training seminars hosted by leading corporations - learn about what they buy, how they source, and how suppliers can compete for opportunities
- Second Tier and MBE-to-MBE Spend business opportunities
- Invitations to private networking and corporate matchmaking and procurement events
- Access to business development resources and scholarships
- Opportunities to compete for prestigious local, regional, and national supplier excellence awards

To me, it seems that the value proposition for an MWBE to be certified is clear; but only a fraction of those eligible actually pursue third party certification from either of these two organizations. Once again, this leaves me asking:

Why?

Too Many Options

For women and minority-owned businesses looking to become suppliers for Corporate America, NMSDC and WBENC are clearly the go-to minority certifying organizations. However, nearly every state and most cities have their own versions of MWBE certification. More often than not, these certifications are free (unlike WBENC and NMSDC). There is also the SBA 8A certification offered by the federal government, as well as the fact that all small businesses can self-certify as disadvantaged business enterprises (DBE) with the federal government. Lastly, many Fortune 500 companies will 'encourage' their MWBEs to pursue NMSDC/WBENC certification, but will often accept many of the other certifications available to the MWBE community.

It Depends on the Business

The beauty of the American capitalist free market economy is that each and every business, minority or not, must make its own decisions that it believes will result in greater sales, lower cost and higher profit margins. In other words, each business should make decisions that are in its best interest.

This is nothing new. Adam Smith, considered to be the father of modern economics, first echoed this sentiment in the *Wealth of Nations*, written in 1776. He wrote specifically about how people, acting in their own self-interest, will ultimately create the betterment of the society as a whole. Smith used the example of a baker to illustrate his point. A baker does not get up early each morning to bake bread solely because of his love for mankind; but because by making bread, he earns an income which allows him to provide food, clothing, and shelter for his family. As a result of each person acting in their own self-interest, to provide for themselves and their families, the goods and services we desire in our economy will be produced.

As a diverse business advocate and supporter, I can suggest what I think would be most beneficial for the success of a diverse business (or any business for that matter), based on years of experience and mounds of research around what other successful diverse businesses have done or have in common. I believe success leaves clues, or as Tony Robbins said in his bestselling book, *Unlimited Power.*

If you want to achieve success, all you need to do is find a way to model those who have already succeeded.

In the end, all businesses must decide to do what is best for them individually, which - in a perfect world - will ultimately be, as Adam Smith says, also in the best interest of society.

Chapter 9

What Do We Really Count and Why?

Numbers are the product of counting. Quantities are the product of measurement. This means that numbers can conceivably be accurate because there is a discontinuity between each integer and the next.

George Bateson

English Anthropologist, Social Scientist and Cyberneticist

I'm a Little Confused, But Don't Tell Anybody

I have tried to start each chapter with a quote that is related to the content of the chapter in some way, shape, or form - and this quote is no exception, but perhaps not for the seemingly obvious reason. To be honest, although this quote sounds good to me, I'm not exactly sure what it means; and I'm not going to say that out loud because I don't want others to know that I don't know. Ironically, that is the way I feel about much of the diverse business spend reporting of many major buying organizations, both public and private. What is included and what is excluded often seems to depend on the company, the industry, and even the area of the country in which the business is buying and selling goods and services. In addition, it seems as if companies with a low percentage of overall spend going to MWSDVBEs report absolute dollars, while others with comparatively small numbers, but with larger portions of their overall spend, report percentages.

As a result, when Company A or Government Agency B stands up and proudly says we spend 21% with MWDVBEs, or we spend $500 million with MWDVBEs, I - like most others - nod my head with no real idea of what they are actually saying. To make matters worse, it is difficult to establish "best practices" because it is hard to make apples-to-apples comparisons between companies, let alone across industries. Like my commentary on the quote I started this chapter with, many others (like me) have confessed that, although the reports sound good, they aren't absolutely sure what's really being said.

Mr. Green, You're Up First

With this as the backdrop, the next topic for discussion had to focus on the calculation of "spend" within the MWSDVBE Supplier Diversity communities. Given that Reggie Layton was our only corporate representative on the panel, a recognized leader in the Supplier Diversity industry, and the fact that the company he represented was a member of the Billion Dollar Roundtable, I knew he would likely be the expert in this area. As a result, I wanted to save him for last on this topic. The Billion Dollar Roundtable was created in 2001 to recognize and pay tribute to major corporations that spent at least $1 billion with minority and woman-owned business enterprises in the past year.

After briefly setting up the topic, I was eager to begin, and turned the mic over to Louis Green. With his trademark "in your face" honesty, he did not let me down, as he said:

"Yeah, of course, corporations do it."

The "it" that Louis was talking about relates to how a major buying organization determines eligible spend. Eligible spend is the denominator, or all of the spend available for bid or competitive sourcing, that an MWSDVBE may be able to go after. For example, some companies may exclude taxes from their eligible spend under the premise that there is only one entity, the government, to which the dollars "spent" on taxes will go. As a result, this will never be competitively bid and should be excluded as a factor in the eligible spend. This argument does make sense, but one of the issues that creates some angst is the liberties major buying organizations may take by adding a host of other goods and services to the list of items excluded from the organizations' eligible spend.

There are many line items that the major buying organizations may not count as part of their eligible spend that include: utilities (gas, water, electric), telephone, payroll and items that only have one source from which they can be bought. The problem is that some major buying organizations do not exclude anything, and some are very liberal in what they choose to exclude from the eligible spend bucket. The issue is not so much what's included, versus what's not included. The bigger issue is the lack of consistency in determining the eligible spend denominator within the Supplier Diversity community.

Louis continued:

"Some do, not all. Some people will say they have business reasons, some people are trying to meet a number for whatever reasons - for contracts, for public face, whatever - others are more serious about their numbers and the integrity of their numbers, and most companies don't treat their minority Supplier Diversity numbers with the same integrity as they will with other numbers. It can be a little soft, a little loose. Reggie, you're looking at me like you might disagree.

I think most companies don't keep good numbers. I doubt if most CEOs, if they had to stand behind their numbers, they wouldn't do it because most *of them are soft numbers. I think the bigger issue, Scott, is really about value, because it's easy for a large corporation - potentially - you can have a shell MBE company doing everything in your system, you have a big number but you aren't adding any value, you're not creating jobs, it's not getting down to communities. It really should be the **impact** of the spend, as opposed to the spend itself. The spend only means so much. If I told you - and I come from a place where we've got lots of companies who do over billions of dollars a year - but it's really about the impact of that spend, and I think we've always been focused on the number and the percentage, and we should measure the impact: the lives transformed, the jobs created in communities. Those numbers - there are some more meaningful numbers.*

Minority Business Think Tank...Cue The BIGGER Discussion

All the while Louis was talking, I noticed Don looking particularly interested in what Louis was saying. So it came as no surprise that, when Louis finished, Don immediately asked him:

"And who measures the numbers?"

Louis and I both answered that the major buying organizations compile and measure their own numbers, which had never really seemed to be a problem to me until Don asked. Don't get me wrong; I still don't think this is an obstacle to progress. However, perhaps there is an opportunity for some standardization across the Supplier Diversity industry about the way in which the MWSDVBE spend numbers are calculated, as well as what ultimately goes into that calculation.

To me, this would be similar to the way major buying organizations keep their books and financial records according to Generally Accepted Accounting Principles (GAAP). Taking it one step further, these financial numbers are periodically reviewed (or audited) by an outside party to ensure their validity and to correct any errors. These errors can be positive or negative, although admittedly, it is the negative errors that often receive the most attention. The auditing of reported Supplier Diversity spend numbers may be far off in the future, but it does not seem unreasonable to think that there could soon be some standardization for the calculation and make-up of these numbers.

After hearing answers from both Louis and me as to who compiles the numbers, Don went on to say:

"You made a great point earlier. You talked about a think tank. Where is that African American think tank in this country? I ask this question all the time. There are a couple of organizations that have economists. I know the National Urban League has a fantastic economist, and I was with her at the last convention. Dr. Wilson - White House Initiative? No previous reference - needs clarity on who he is. But I ask this question all the time: Where in America is there a group of men and women whose sole purpose is to measure these things, whether it be in the private sector or not. We want to see what impact the minority programs are having.

We want to measure the public sector, and now we will have a message, so when we do hire our lobbyist - to my right - we will have a message, because we've got good numbers. I ask this question all the time: Where are the numbers? Who is our think tank? Where is our think tank? Other groups have think tanks, plenty of think tanks on the other side, right? Where are our numbers?"

Obviously, the questions that Donald Cravins asked are relevant to why *The BIGGER Discussion* was created. They also undergird the rationale for founding the parent organization, The Institute for Thought Diversity. The concept of a minority business think tank that can measure the impact of the minority business community on the larger community (be it from the support organizations, major buying organizations or the MWSDVBE community itself) was of particular interest to the founders of The Institute. In fact, through *The BIGGER Discussion,* The Institute has already completed several studies designed to investigate and answer these very questions about the relevance and importance of the economic impact of the minority business community on the overall economy. For those of you wanting to learn more about these studies, they can be found at www.thebiggerdiscussion.com.

Once Don finished his remarks, Louis responded:

"And that would open the platform for MBEs. This is the tax revenue we're putting into your community, this is what we're creating in your district. When you do that it empowers you, it empowers the MBEs to do lots of stuff, and helps you make a stronger case. It helps Reggie in his job, right?"

A Model for What Could Be

As if on cue, Dick Huebner jumped right in to follow up on what was being said:

"So I can say from a local level, 20 years into this field, I have never used the numbers that the corporation has reported to me. Because they weren't comparable. I couldn't compare them against each other. They weren't credible, frankly. They were reporting people that they thought were minority businesses.

About six years ago, we went to an effort where we now send them the list of firms and say 'Write in the column next to the list the amount you spent with that firm.' If they're not on the list, they don't count. Now I can do that at the local level, but then that gives me a wealth of information because I can marry that up to the database, and I can find out what fields we are excelling in, what are we overcrowded in, where are the opportunity areas for minority business that we need to begin moving people to?

I think, to the credit of a lot of our corporations in Houston - particularly in the oil and gas industry - where they've said 'okay most of our spend is in downstream, most of our spend with minority firms is in downstream, but there's a huge opportunity in upstream but we don't have many minority firms.' So there is a concerted effort to try to move some firms who have achieved excellence in downstream operations to the upstream, where there's more money and more opportunity. Having those metrics, locally, that justify our existence, but more importantly empower us to 1) recognize companies who are really doing it, and 2) be credible as the authority of minority business development, and 3) flesh out the opportunities. What's the reality and what's the opportunity?"

As I said at the beginning of this book, Richard Huebner is an icon within the Supplier Diversity world. The Houston Minority Supplier Development Council (HMSDC) has won the prestigious NMSDC Council of the Year award more times than I can remember, and under Huebner's leadership, they continue to set the bar in terms of programs and trainings offered, position and respect in the community, and corporate member and MBE participation. Therefore, it comes as no surprise that the HMSDC would continue to be above the curve when compared to the rest of the industry in terms of the calculation and reporting of MBE spend by their corporate members. Could Huebner's model be replicated across the country? Possibly.

Now it was time to hear from Marquis Miller and, as I said earlier, *The BIGGER Discussion* had indeed morphed into a discussion among the thought leaders on the stage. So with simply a head nod as prompting, I indicated to Marquis that his time was now to weigh in on this subject.

"In the context of this panel, subtitled 'The Future of Supplier Diversity,' it's really having more diversity in thought and application of the processes that really make up the endgame; which is to take, as Dick mentions,

those firms that have this successful downstream and develop them so they can do business upstream. That's essentially the essence of our 40 years of focusing on supplier development. There are organizations that do business development, and some of those organizations operate with the think tank mindset. There are chambers that are focused on advocating for those businesses, but it's probably safe to say that every business is not a supplier. So the focus on how you now develop those suppliers is really how you start to drive the metrics, because that's what the companies are paying attention to. How are these collections of businesses going to help us with our corporate goals and objectives?"

Reginald K. Layton Unleashed

I looked over at Reggie, and he looked as if he were about to burst if I waited any longer before allowing his voice to be heard on the subject of MWSDBE spend counting. On a few occasions, Reggie and I had some brief 'water cooler' discussions on the subject of spend, so I knew this was one of his sweet spots and subjects about which he was very passionate. Once again, I listened with an ear to learn as Reggie said:

"So Scott, you asked a question about what we call 'excludables' in the Supplier Diversity world. What do you take out of the calculation so that your numbers look better? In Johnson Controls' case, our program, our initiative, our efforts, our processes are only 16 years old. So in my book, we're novices at this, we're young in doing this. So there are a lot of bad habits that we never picked up, we didn't know that people excluded things. I didn't find that out until I was in the job for eight years. I was like, 'You exclude capital equipment? Really? Why would you do that?'

So we don't exclude anything but salaries, taxes, and contributions. Everything else is fair game. Now what I hear from my colleagues is, 'Well, there are industries where there are no minorities' and I say 'How do you know that? How do you know that?' And then they say 'Well there are no aluminum smelters' and I say 'Well, you know what? We had that situation in our battery group. There were no lead smelters, we thought, until we checked.'

Every day, minority companies and minority management teams are buying existing companies or forming companies. You can't say let's exclude something in the calculation because you believe that they aren't there. It's our job as Supplier Diversity professionals to check. The other thing that's the answer to this is you don't exclude things if you're buying it from a company that's part of the calculation. Then it's all about integrity.

We don't do this calculation on percentages; our projects are denominated in dollars. How much is this project worth? A million dollars, not 10 percent - what is that? So there's a whole orientation on the calculation: projects are denominated in dollars, work is denominated in dollars, the metrics are denominated in dollars, the goals are in dollars, everything's in dollars.

Since we are going to have numbers-based metrics, let's deal with that. I was looking at the numbers: You heard me say that we're going to end the fiscal year 2012 at $1.8 billion. Okay, so that's 565 minority and women-owned companies, 80 percent of those are minority-owned companies that are certified. We've got another 300 that are alleged that don't count. I looked at the number of employees they have: 93,000 employees. That's 93,000 jobs. So your point about having an advocacy mechanism in the public sector is important because you would provide that type of data; 93,000 jobs are depending on these 560 diverse companies doing services for just Johnson Controls.

The other thing: How do you get this type of information? The councils, NMSDC, they have to push the idea of surveillance systems. You cannot run a program managing 560 plus diverse companies on a spreadsheet. And I didn't mention that there are another 1,100 in the queue, with 2,500 buyers all over the country - and that's not counting the ones not sitting in the United States. You cannot do it without surveillance systems where you could pick up this data and have an intelligent conversation with your management and the public sector.

The other thing: cascading the requirements to other corporations. In our world we call this 'second tier.' Yeah, you could give them a percentage, but you could say 'No, I want a solution from you. I want a solution from you, Mr. Prime, that involves women and minority-owned companies. Eighty-eight of JCI's primes rose to the occasion. When I looked at their numbers, they only spent $111 million—that's not much compared to our $1.8 billion. But they managed 963 minority and women-owned companies with all the jobs that that brings to the table.

So my point is, when you deal with excludables - you pull on that thread - there's a lot to it. You need to have surveillance systems, you need to promote an organization's integrity around what the numbers are, killing this idea of excluding things to make the percentage look better. Don't even deal with percentages, deal with dollars and projects and what are they."

Whew! Reginald K. Layton had a lot to say. As moderator, I remember my head spinning during this part of *The BIGGER Discussion,* as he seamlessly jumped from one subject to the next (all related) concerning the way in which MWSDVBE spend is counted by major buying organizations (specifically Johnson Controls, Inc.). Reggie was literally bouncing off his seat as he bubbled over with enthusiasm to answer this question. I was truly moved by his passion for Supplier Diversity, and nowhere was it more evident than when he answered this question.

There is so much to be dissected and analyzed in what Reggie said that his comments alone could likely be enough for their own *BIGGER Discussion.* In fact, if you look at the video again (as I hope you will or have already done) or read the 'Bonus' transcript (which is included in its entirety at the end of this book), you will see that this part of the conversation actually continued for another 3-4 minutes, and we still didn't cover all the issues.

Chapter 9.1

In Chasing Spend, Have We Lost Sight of the Real Goal?

One of the lessons that I grew up with was to always stay true to yourself and never let what somebody else says distract from your goals. And so when I hear about negative and false attacks, I really don't invest any energy in them because I know who I am.

Michelle Obama

First Lady of the United States

I have many friends and mentors in all aspects of my life, but particularly in my chosen field of Supplier Diversity and minority business development. One of them is Dr. Melvin Gravely II. I would say that, over the last decade or so, he has been among the most prolific and consistent writers and speakers on the subject of Supplier Diversity and minority business development. Although Mel and I may differ on some views concerning minority business development, the one area in which he has had the most influence on my line of thinking is in the area of MWSDVBE spend. In this section, I unapologetically borrow liberally from Dr. Gravely in formulating my opinions on this subject, and I am sure that those of you who are familiar with Dr. Gravely's work may notice the similarities. I am okay with that because, as Voltaire said:

Originality is nothing but judicious imitation. The most original writers borrowed one from another.

Impact or Just Spend? So Far it is Just Spend

How robust a major buying organization's Supplier Diversity program is performing is quite often based on one, and only one, metric: its total dollar spend with the diverse business community. Third-party organizations will issue report cards to judge it, there are awards, lists and events to recognize it, government agencies mandating it, and questionable business structures being set up to achieve it. Please do not misunderstand me, I think spend goals serve an important purpose, as in 'that which is measured gets done, managed or improved.' For the sake of convenience, measuring spend is simple, growth can be easily quantified and tracked, and goals can be painlessly set.

My issue with the laser focus on measuring the dollars spent in procuring goods and services from minority suppliers is that we are not measuring the economic *impact* of that spend. Earlier in *The BIGGER Discussion*, Donald Cravins lamented the fact that minorities are still disproportionately being incarcerated, likely to be below the poverty line, have less education, receive subpar healthcare and, in general, suffer from a lower standard of living in comparison with their non-minority counterparts. This is indeed an unfortunate irony, given the fact that the original intent of the various Supplier Diversity initiatives was to, at least partially, serve as a means to eradicate some of these socio-economic woes experienced by the disenfranchised minority sectors of the population.

Focus on Spend Makes it Easier to Lose Sight of the Real Goal

The seeming fascination with how much a major buying organization spends with minority business enterprises as the primary measure of success could be distracting from the real goal of a successful Supplier Diversity initiative. That is if the real goal is to develop a base of competitive diverse suppliers, with the understanding that these businesses will in turn uplift their underdeveloped communities by investing back into those communities.

This reinvestment will make itself manifest in more jobs providing a living wage, and better public services and schools as a result of greater positive contributions to the tax base by these minority businesses and those they employ. I could go on and on with the benefits, but I think you get the general idea.

Unfortunately, these positive results for the minority communities in general - and the national economy (income generation, job creation and tax revenue) as a whole - are rarely, if ever, mentioned when talking about Supplier Diversity metrics. By far, the metric that is most often used for measuring the success of a corporation's Supplier Diversity program is the total number of dollars spent with these diverse businesses.

If we pretend that corporations do not care about the impact their spend with MWSDVBEs has on the community, or their customer's requirements to have a program, is there still a reason to have a Supplier Diversity program? The answer is *yes*, but only if Supplier Diversity is seen as a strategic initiative used by the corporation to foster increased competition between suppliers that ultimately results in lower costs and greater value. In other words, *how and why* major buying organizations spend with diverse suppliers, and the impact of that spend on the buying organization and the community, should be as important as *how much* they spend.

The Focus on Spend Encourages Questionable Behavior

In general, it seems that if a major buying organization spends X amount of dollars with diverse businesses, they are fulfilling the mission; and I would be remiss if I did not acknowledge that for many organizations this is indeed true. Please do not think that I am saying that achieving spend goals with MWSDVBEs, creating competitive diverse businesses in the process, and ultimately positively impacting the community are necessarily mutually exclusive. They are not.

That said, I must also acknowledge that when a major buying organization passes products or services through a MWSDVBE-owned distributor only to be able to "count" the spend, the mission of the Supplier Diversity initiative on any level other than reaching a spend goal, is likely not being fulfilled. In this case, the diverse firm adds little value to the transaction and grows no capacity, but the major buying organization did spend more with a diverse supplier. Did they develop a competitive, sustainable diverse supplier that will have long lasting positive economic impact on their communities in the process? I doubt it.

Let's Do It the Right Way

As I said earlier, there are many corporations and government entities that are increasing the amount of business they do with MWSDVBEs, and developing more competitive diverse suppliers in the process. The question is: how can we get more organizations doing this?

The answer is obvious. Let's begin by incorporating other metrics for success in addition to spend with diverse suppliers, and let's weigh those metrics comparably to spend. Impact metrics - such as the tax impact on the community, revenue generated by the MWSDVBE, and jobs created as a result of the diverse business getting the opportunity - would be a good start.

Let's not put the entire onus unfairly on the major buying organizations. The diverse business community should also be measuring how much they are growing in terms of contracts, capacity and profit margins, versus industry standards. Support organizations should also be able to measure the economic impact of the diverse business community they serve through the lens of job creation, tax revenue and income generation.

I will say again, I understand that how much is spent with minority businesses is a critical metric, and should likely still be at the top of the list; but it cannot be the only measure that matters. The goal is to empower and improve socio-economically challenged and impoverished communities by engaging historically underutilized businesses that can be developed into competitive and capable suppliers.

This is the core mission of all Supplier Diversity initiatives. The development and maintenance of competitive, capable suppliers competing on a level playing field regardless of race, creed, religion, gender, or sexual orientation is what success looks like. Competitive, capable suppliers provide value to their customers, their shareholders and their communities. These are the outcomes that are sustainable, and the only ones worth our investment of time, talent and treasure.

The BIGGER Discussion

Final Thoughts

Chapter 10

Conclusion

Here's to the crazy ones. The misfits. The rebels. The troublemakers. The round pegs in the square holes. The ones who see things differently. They're not fond of rules. And they have no respect for the status quo. You can quote them, disagree with them, glorify or vilify them. About the only thing you can't do is ignore them. Because they change things. They push the human race forward. And while some may see them as the crazy ones, we see genius. Because the people who are crazy enough to think they can change the world, are the ones who do.

Steve Jobs

Co-founder, Chairman, and CEO of Apple Inc.

Supplier Diversity Needs Fixing

In 1997, after Steve Jobs had returned to the helm of a struggling Apple, he felt the need to reinforce the company's core values to the public. At the time, there were no new innovative products being introduced at Apple because a restructuring of the company was taking place. However, Jobs knew that in order to move the company forward, he first had to re-establish the core values around which Apple was built, both internally within the company and externally with the general public. In his mind, he correctly understood that the products being offered were not as significant as making sure everyone understood the "why" around which Apple was built. If you can get people to understand your "why", and buy in to your vision, they will almost always likely buy your products (in the case of Apple) or support your cause.

Steve Jobs did just that with the now famous 1997 "Think Different" campaign. The words of this ad provide a perfect segue for me to talk to you about what *The BIGGER Discussion* is really all about in terms of Supplier Diversity or, in other words, get you to understand our "why".

By now, you know who the founders of *The BIGGER Discussion* are: Phala Mire, Al Williams and me, Scott Vowels. You also know that we were able to catch lightning in a bottle when the YouTube production was seen by more than 32,000 people. But that is just one offering from *The BIGGER Discussion* as an entity. It is not what *The BIGGER Discussion* is all about, nor does it simply tell you why we had the panel discussion in the first place.

We collectively decided that, despite the fact that the Supplier Diversity industry today is indeed a multi-billion dollar enterprise, it is in need of fixing. We wholeheartedly acknowledge that there are quite a few minority, women, veteran, gay, lesbian, and transgender small businesses that are extremely successful in terms of revenue, jobs created, community involvement, tax impact, or any imaginable measure of success by which a business is judged. Many of these businesses owe all, or at least a significant portion of their success, to the Supplier Diversity industry. So, how can I say that we believe the industry needs fixing?

The Original Goals of the Supplier Diversity Industry...

At its core, there are two stated objectives or intended outcomes of the Supplier Diversity industry. These are the same goals and outcomes that were articulated in the early 1970's, when Supplier Diversity as a movement (and later an industry) came into being with the signing of Executive Orders 11428 and 11625 by then President Richard Nixon.

The first goal was to enable (and help create) some fully capable minority businesses that could not only compete, but also succeed, in a big way in the United States ultra-competitive free market, capitalistic environment. Supplier Diversity programs were intended to do this by helping to eradicate artificial barriers to entry for a fully capable business that had been based on non-market driven forces such as race, creed, religion, gender, national origin and sexual orientation.

These successful diverse businesses, now allowed to compete unencumbered and win contracting opportunities within industries in which they were previously not allowed to participate, would in turn reinvest their revenues back into their socio-economically challenged communities in a variety of ways. For one, the owners of the MWSDVBE businesses would be able to pay a competitive living wage to their employees. This would raise the level of the middle class in the diverse communities that were previously socio-economically distressed and impoverished, when compared to their majority counterparts.

In other words, one of the goals of the Supplier Diversity initiative early on was wealth creation, and self-empowerment in communities in which neither of these conditions existed in a large enough quantity to make a difference. The empowerment of these communities to help themselves, and not rely on others (including the government), would be made manifest in the communities' ability to solve the problems associated with economic blight - including crime, poor educational systems, poverty and an overall sense of hopelessness and apathy. This is the "why" behind the Supplier Diversity movement, and I believe that somewhere along the way, we (like Apple prior to 1997) need to re-visit it, and I suggest sooner as opposed to later.

As my friend, Dr. Mel Gravely, so eloquently and simply stated in his latest book, *The Capacity to Succeed,* when talking about the goals of Supplier Diversity and the minority business development industry:

Truth is wealth, and this is what we really want. Wealth creation is the outcome of business success, and business success means we've built a business capable of serving customers. Plus, wealth-creating businesses hire people, invest in communities, and participate in philanthropy (delivering more social value). On average, minorities are more prone to giving than whites. In some cases, they give up to 25 percent more, according to "Cultures of Giving," a report by the W.K. Kellogg Foundation (January 2012).

... Are Not Being Met

"I'm 40 years old, and since the time I was 19, I've seen African American boys kill each other every day. In this city of New Orleans, we have as bad of an epidemic as we've ever had; in the city of Baton Rouge, we've got probably the worst epidemic we've ever had. And I am now convinced, as a former politician and as someone who used to run for office and thought 'I could save the day,' I am now convinced that the only way we can really raise ourselves out of this is through economics. We've always said that. But, Dick, I am now convinced that the only way we can make our communities better is to have thriving African American businesses in those communities hiring people, creating jobs and creating good family models."

These were the words of Don Cravins. With his heartfelt, grittily honest assessment of where we are in terms of actual results from the hard work of those in the Supplier Diversity profession today - and those who have gone before us - Don painstakingly detailed what I would use as proof to say that we have a long way to go in fulfilling the true mission of the Supplier Diversity industry. He spoke specifically of the African American community, but I promise you (and there is an overwhelming amount of readily available research to substantiate my point) that this is a problem in almost every socio-economically challenged minority community in the United States.

We Are Crazy at The BIGGER Discussion... and So Are You

... *"Because the people who are crazy enough to think they can change the world are the ones who do".*

I began this last section of the book with the entire transcript from the 1997 "Think Different" Apple commercial, but it is the last line that best encapsulates what *The BIGGER Discussion* as an organization, is truly all about. We see that the promise of a brighter future for all Americans is not being realized, as was the original intent of the Supplier Diversity initiatives that began some forty years ago. We can see it in the facts that:

- The lowest earning 23,303,064 Americans combined make 36 percent less than the highest earning 2,915 Americans do.
- 49.7 million Americans are living in poverty.
- The wealthiest one percent of all Americans have a greater net worth than the bottom 90 percent combined.
- More than 60% of the people in prison are now racial and ethnic minorities (Doctorow, 2013)

When Al and Phala originally approached me with the concept, I must admit I was skeptical at first, to say the least. They had been developing the concept for several months, and had a vision for where they wanted *The BIGGER Discussion* to go, and what they wanted it and its parent organization, The Institute for Thought Diversity to be.

In my opinion, the foresight and vision displayed by them must not be taken for granted - nor should it be overlooked - given the success of the panel discussion, which is only the first offering of *The BIGGER Discussion* as an organization, or better yet, a movement. The two of them are a living testimony to the oft-used Bible verse:

Without a vision, the people will perish. Proverbs 29:18 KJV

The *BIGGER Discussion,* through The Institute for Thought Diversity, will continue to push the envelope to enable a meaningful dialogue around socio-economic issues facing historically disenfranchised sectors of the larger community. Think tanks, thought-provoking and informative publications, economic impact studies, seminars, dynamic speakers, and so much more are all components of The *BIGGER Discussion* that will be rolled out in the very near future. My co-founders are ambitious visionaries in every sense of the word, and I am truly privileged to be along for the ride on what I know will be a great and worthwhile adventure (yes I did say adventure and not endeavor). And the good news is: there is room for you.

We at *The BIGGER Discussion,* like so many before us, are just crazy enough to believe that we can change the world - starting with the honest, meaningful, respectful, informative, results-oriented dialogue that took place on August 23, 2012 in New Orleans.

What's more, we believe that there are many more of us out there who believe the same thing. Finally, if you have stayed with me this far, then I believe YOU are the person I am talking about! I invite you to join my colleagues and me at *The BIGGER Discussion* in daring to dream of a better future, working to bring that dream to life, and together changing the world for the better.

The BIGGER Discussion

The Transcript

Bonus Section

Discussion is an exchange of knowledge; an argu-
ment is an exchange of ignorance.
Robert Quillen
American Journalist and Humorist

I started this book by telling you about the numerous times that I have been stopped and asked questions about *The BIGGER Discussion – The Future of Supplier Diversity.* I gave a few examples of the typical questions that were asked, but one that I left out was:

"Where can I get a copy of the Transcript?"

Well, ask no more. On the next twenty or so pages, you will find every word of the video viewed more than 32,000 times on YouTube. The transcript appears in its entirety, except for the editing of a few of the unnecessary 'Uhhs, Ums and Ahs.' As I said in the beginning of this book, I picked out a few of my favorite moments from *The BIGGER Discussion* (which was not easy) and focused this book on those. However, I would love to know what your favorite moments were, as well as those moments where you could sense that something was going on behind the scenes that might not have been planned. If there is any juicy scoop I could give you about those moments, I promise I will.

I have viewed the YouTube video hundreds of times, and read the transcript just as many. Every time, I have found something interesting that I had overlooked in the first 100 times. In fact, if I were to write this book today, it would likely look completely different than it looks today, in terms of my favorite moments.

So with that, I encourage you to read the transcript, think, take another look at the video on YouTube (as well as *The BIGGER Discussion 2,* also now available on You Tube), and enjoy.

The BIGGER Discussion - The Future of Supplier Diversity

New Orleans Convention Center
August 23, 2012

Participants:
Phala Mire - President, Louisiana MSDC
Scott Vowels - President, Northern California MSDC
Louis Green - President, Michigan MSDC
Donald Cravins - Staff Director and Chief Counsel, U.S. Senate Committee on Small Business and Entrepreneurship
Marquis Miller - Vice President, National Minority Supplier Development Council (NMSDC)
Reginald Layton - Director of Supplier Diversity, Johnson Controls Inc.
Richard Huebner - President, Houston MSDC

Phala Mire: Welcome to Gateway 2012. I want to thank everybody for being here this morning. This is the opening of our conference. For those of you who have been with us in the past, you know we're doing things a little differently this year. We have been talking and we are constantly looking for ways to make this conference and events like this more meaningful for you, more productive. And so in discussions with other Council presidents throughout the NSMDC network, with conversations that we have with people that we work with day-to-day, we felt that there was a need to have a discussion. And so we call this *"The BIGGER Discussion."* So I want to welcome you to our general session this morning: *The BIGGER Discussion on The Future of Supplier Diversity.* In front of you, you have a very distinguished panel of people, and I'm going to introduce them in a minute. But I do want to just reiterate what we printed in our program book, and that is that we - and I mean collectively "we" - believe in the power of dialogue to change attitudes, actions and business practices. And so that's what this is today - this is a discussion event from experts in various fields. We have people from the public sector, people from the private sector, people from associations and organizations - all here with a point of view. They're going to tackle some pretty hard-hitting questions, and we hope that the dialogue that is then provoked is going to stimulate you all to have conversations outside of this session, so that this sets the tone for the next two days - which we have a jam-packed session of things that will be going on. I'll tell you a little bit about that after the session is over. For those of you who have been following and paying close attention to how we have this set up, we are streaming this session live, so we also have people viewing the session from their desks from their home computers. And they'll be Tweeting in questions as well. So right now, I'm going to introduce our panel and I'm going to start with our moderator for this session. Our moderator is Scott Vowels; he is the President of the Northern California Minority Supplier Development Council. Next to Scott, we have Louis Green; he is the President of the Michigan Minority Supplier Development Council. Next to Louis, we have Donald Cravins, who is the Director and Chief Counsel of the U.S. Senate Committee on Small Business and Entrepreneurship. Next to Mr. Cravins, Marquis Miller, the Vice President of the National Minority Supplier Development Council. We have Reginald Layton, who is the Director of Supplier Diversity for Johnson Controls. And last, but certainly not least, we have Richard Huebner, President of the Houston Minority Supplier Development Council. Ladies and gentlemen, our panel. Now you'll notice that I didn't spend a lot of time telling you about them. Their bios are in the program book, and I know many of you will be having conversations with them, and many of you already know them. This conversation, right now, is about to get off, and we want them to have a conversation among each other, and we want you to feel free to participate. If you have your cell phones - and we know you do - put them on silent or vibrate. If you have a Twitter account, go ahead and feel free to Tweet your questions as well. We want audience participation, but we won't be taking live questions from the floor. So we are doing this interactively, and certainly I need to thank both Google and MSF Global, one of our MBEs, for helping us set up all the technology that was required to get this done. So thank you all in advance, and I look forward to a great *BIGGER Discussion*.

Scott Vowels: So, again, my name is Scott Vowels. I run the Northern California Minority Supplier Development Council and first off, I want to apologize. I did not realize how bright the lights were, so the gleaming off my head if it blinds any of you, it's not personal. Also, I would be remiss if we didn't thank the LAMSDC and their staff, because this is going to be a great conference. And also their Board of Directors that is empowering them to have this discussion. So hopefully, this will be the first of many discussions going forward. So I would like to say a brief thank you to staff and the Board for allowing this to happen. I'm going to ask one favor from the audience: If we're truly going to have a *BIGGER Discussion*, then I'm going to ask you for a minute or two, or for two hours - however long we have you in here - if you don't mind if we suspend the political correctness that we're always surrounded by when we have these discussions. Is that okay with the audience? Okay, because my panel said they wanted to, but I had to make sure that you guys were okay with it. So we'll start off...and here's how we're going to frame the discussion: one of my favorite comedians is Paul Mooney. He was a writer for Richard Pryor, and he said some crazy things that aren't necessarily appropriate; but one of the things he said that resonated with me was he said that you were either running free or running scared, and the question was "how are you running?" So I think we have been walking cautiously around some of the concepts of Supplier Diversity, not necessarily running, but hopefully now we're going to start running more free, and hopefully this is the beginning of many discussions. The other thing I'm going to ask this audience to do is provide feedback to the Council, provide feedback to anybody that you can that you want this discussion to continue—if it's meaningful at all. Now if it falls on its face, then just forget I was even up here. So now we'll dive right into it, and this will be the last you'll hear from me. We have our first African American President, a minority in the office. Let's forget the fact that he's African American for a second. He's a minority in the office so I'm wondering since we have that, do we even really need Supplier Diversity anymore? Let's just start off with that. And I have to give credit to Mr. Cravins because he's the one who got me thinking about that. So I'd like to hear from everyone on the panel on that one, then we'll dive into some of the others. So Mr. Green, you are first.

Louis Green: No. Don't need it anymore.

Donald Cravins: Fair enough. Thank you all for allowing me to be here today, and thank the leadership for allowing me to be here. I'm the government guy, and although I know a lot of the panelists here today are going to talk about business, they're going to talk about Supplier Diversity, the reason I wanted to be part of this discussion is because I think, as someone who helps the United States Senate craft legislation - many to deal with the 8A program and other preference programs, the women's program, our vets and disabled program - I watch what goes on in the Supplier Diversity field because, again, if we don't need Supplier Diversity, do we need preference programs in the federal government? I disagree; I think we do need them. But I am glad we are having this discussion and I think, since the election of President Obama, I have found that - particularly in minority folks, particularly African Americans - we fall in one of three categories, and because we fall into one of those categories it has made these discussions a necessity. We fall into the category that we've got an African American president and no, now we don't need Supplier Diversity and we don't need preference programs. There's a school of thought that we made some progress with the election of an African American president, but there's still more to go. And then there's some folks who think it doesn't mean anything, that we're just in the same boat that we were in 20 years ago. I'm kind of in the second school of thought - it's obviously progress, my kids are seeing something that I never ever, ever thought I was going to get to see, a family that looks like them in the White House – however, ladies and gentlemen, I will tell you I'm glad we're having this discussion because it does make it increasingly hard to justify the need for these programs... and even worse than that, when this presidency is over, I think particularly in the government you're going to also see a rush to get rid of all these programs. You had a president who looked like you for eight years, you guys made strides and gains during those eight years, we've got to take things away from you, when we all know that's not necessarily true. And so I'm glad we're having this discussion, I do think we need Supplier Diversity, but I can tell you from a government standpoint I think there's still very much a need. At least the testimony we hear at the United States Senate Small Business Committeeis that programs like the 8A program, programs that help minorities and African Americans, Hispanic Americans, we still need that. If you look at the wealth gap in this country to this day, African Americans, Hispanic Americans, still our median wealth is here, and other Asian Americans and White Americans, it's up here. I think as long as you have that disparity in wealth and median incomes, you've got to have programs that help us.

Scott Vowels: Marquis?

Marquis Miller: I would say yes, and I would say yes for two specific reasons. One, I don't know that having the first minority president is necessarily connected to the need to have Supplier Diversity. I do think a focus on minority supplier development is essential for the very same reasons that Mr. Cravins suggested, but I also think that when you think about what's good and proper about diversity and for the number of years that Corporate America focused on being more diverse in their hiring and in their community engagement, just like any good stool you have to have a third leg. And that third leg happens to be diverse suppliers. It's really no different when you think about all the ways diversity inclusion is a part of the fabric of our country, irrespective of who the president is, and before there was a minority president in the White House there were good, strong diversity programs and I would argue that, on that basis alone, Supplier Diversity should continue to be included.

Louis Green: Scott, can I elaborate on my "no" so people can understand where I'm coming from?

Scott Vowels: We're going to hear from Reggie and then you. We're going to come back to you because I am dying to know why you said no. Go ahead, Reggie.

Reginald Layton: So Scott, I think having an African American president is excellent. It's one of the greatest things I think the United States has ever done. Notwithstanding that though, Supplier Diversity is needed because of different reasons. It's about economically equipping historically underutilized population groups. So even though President Obama is in the White House that doesn't change the fact that you have disparity in economics with minority groups and with women and with people who are driving market expansions for corporations. And you also have the need because - there's the diversity angle - of innovation, and if you don't have inclusiveness in your supply chain, you risk as a corporation missing opportunities to develop new products, to be able to make inroads in new markets, both here in the United States and around the world, so you do yourself a disservice by not having Supplier Diversity. So I appreciate what we have with President Obama - but this isn't about how it looks, this isn't about the cosmetic and the picture looking right, this is about the dollars and cents that are in minority and women decision makers' pockets and in their communities.

Scott Vowels: I am so glad I am not following Reggie. Go ahead, Dick.

Richard Huebner: And I'm sad I am! I believe that Supplier Diversity is needed more today than it's ever been needed, and for a lot of the reasons Reggie just articulated. It's not so much about race as it is about economics. Supplier Diversity was established to create viable businesses in minority communities to fuel the growth of those businesses with corporate expenditures, so that as they grew they would create jobs, economic self-sufficiency, a broadened tax base for the community, lower tax rates and increased spending for everyone's goods and services. In essence, creating an economic engine in those disadvantaged communities that would then fuel the growth of that community, the city, state and the nation. That's desperately needed today as we try as a country, as a world, to rebound, to regrow our economy. The fact is that there is a growing gap between the 'haves' - largely white - and the 'have-nots' - almost exclusively people of color. That gap has to be corrected and it has to be done in a free enterprise system. We need to involve people actively; we need to be proactive, if you will, about involving everybody in the free enterprise system. It really isn't working as well as we think it is. Yes, race relations may be at a better keel right now, but that can change if the economics don't also change. So I believe that Supplier Diversity is needed more than anytime in the 28 years I have been doing this.

Scott Vowels: Now we're circling back.

Louis Green: Thank you. So first of all, President Obama - a black president - has nothing to do with Supplier Diversity or Supplier Diversity programs, first of all. Second of all, I don't believe in programs. Programs are by their nature temporary, finite and aren't in the fabric of something. Thirdly, I think folks really should be on minority business as opposed to Supplier Diversity because it is about economics, and it shouldn't even be a minority business program, it should be a majority business program. People of color are just steps away from being the majority of the population of this country; ergo, it's going to drive the engine of this economy. We have already lost the position as being the first-rated economy in the world, that's down to China. If we don't want to go down to third or fourth or fifth, the active involvement of people of color who are going to drive, who are going to be the decision-makers in corporations, who are going to be the suppliers to businesses, who are going to be the businesses themselves, needs to be a focus - a very intentional focus - of empowering them to do some things. So when you say Supplier Diversity program, that to me just weakens something that's very, very important. We don't look at it as strategic; we look at it as something to do. It gets pushed off in PR departments of corporations. People can put an ad and say, "We care about businesses", and it looks good and doesn't mean a damn thing. So I have a problem with the whole concept of Supplier Diversity, and especially you had the nerve to link it to President Obama. So my answer, no.

Scott Vowels: I had the nerve? So the other rule we're going to have up here: there will be no more profanity, and as I can see this is getting personal there will be no talking about each other's momma. Alright, so one of the things I find whether it's a minority business, Supplier Diversity.

Louis Green: But they aren't interchangeable, Scott.

Scott Vowels: However we want to couch it, I think the pool is getting diluted. I think that there are many more groups being gathered into that pool, and whether it's Corporate America or the government sector, the spend, the goals haven't changed that much but the pool is becoming increasingly diluted. So when we're talking about The Future of Supplier Diversity—and we're looking at 2050 when we're going to be a majority-minority country—then does it flip all the way around? We're talking about The Future of it. This time we'll start down there with Dick.

Richard Huebner: Well I'm greatly concerned about the trend that we've seen over a good number of years now, particularly at the government level, to broaden the definition of minority or whatever it's called now - historically underutilized or whatever - to include everyone. So we've been able to make the statement "yes we're growing in our spend", but are we really achieving the objectives we set out to achieve 40 years ago? I don't think so. We still see African American businesses, as an example, languishing way behind everyone else. But yet we can point to our success in doing business with the women, with all the other disenfranchised groups, and I'm not saying there shouldn't be a focus on including them. If that's justified, certainly we should. But let's not take our eye off the ball and give in to the tendency of being able to make it easier to report progress when true progress, at least on some fronts, is not being made.

Scott Vowels: Reggie.

Reginald Layton: On the one hand, you have Supplier Diversity, which is a set of processes by which an organization would seek to do business with historically underutilized population groups. So, on the one hand I'm happy that we're being precise in our terms. You have the public sector with a set of processes that are really political and legislative, they deemed who was historically underutilized.

Then you have the corporate sector where they are doing it for a different set of reasons, and we shouldn't assume that the two sets of communities have the same reasons. One might be political, one might be market-oriented, the other might be supply chain efficiency-oriented. That being said, when you expand the pool of classifications as it's called, I agree with Dick. You have to know what you're trying to do. You have to be precise in your terms. Do you deal with an environment where the decisions are made by women? So be precise, have a Supplier Diversity program that supports women business enterprises. Do you have a program where you're trying to diversify the base because you see that minority group members are growing not only in demographics but in wealth, they are better educated now as business owners than they ever were, does that present an advantage to you? Then you design your set of processes, your program, so you go after that particular opportunity. So my point is, on the one hand I'm glad that we're being precise in our terms; on the other hand, I agree with Dick. Whatever you do to go after those particular strategies, there should be some reasoning behind it and there should be some gain in what you're doing. So it's not about growing the pool and getting the numbers up; it's about what are you trying to do and are you successful in doing it? And you measure your progress based on what you're trying to do. If you're trying to increase spend, fine. If you're trying to increase the quantity of a particular type of supplier, fine. If you're trying to diversify where they are located, you would have a strategy to move suppliers around, or if it's about growing them internationally. So I think in this regard it's not that you're widening the pool - it's what are you trying to do with these groups that are historically underutilized? That's how we do it.

Scott Vowels: Marquis, anything to add?

Marquis Miller: I don't think anyone would argue that more diversity isn't good and proper. I do think that, as the pie has gotten sliced in multiple ways, the fact that there was a pie baked in the first place to provide opportunity is something that we're steadfastly committed to. The National Minority Supplier Development Council is going to mark its 40th anniversary this year, and we were chartered to focus on ethnic minorities: Asian, Black, Hispanic and Native American-owned and operated businesses. We truly believe that it's important to recognize the significance of diversity, but we're going to stay focused on our charter because we think that, to Dick and Reggie's point, it's really the economic impact that we're interested in - and ensuring that there are opportunities to develop and then deliver that economic impact so that communities of color can be better at participating in the American economy.

Scott Vowels: Go ahead, Don.

Donald Cravins: In the governmental programs, you've seen the same dilution. We've seen the definition of minority change and, as you raised, a lot of that has been political - and I'm glad you raised the political question. I am one of two African American committee chiefs of staff in the United States Senate and one of four in the entire Congress. And I will tell you, ladies and gentlemen, I can count on one hand the amount of times that I have been visited by African American folks who said "Donald we are here today to talk about we do not want to dilute the definition any further of the 8A program." I can't count on one hand the number of times I've been visited by other groups, and I'm an African American. I would think African American people would think my door is open. It is political, and I think even with Supplier Diversity, you see things being diluted, we have an obligation - those of us who are African American or those of us who are for or against it - have an obligation to participate in that process, whether it's political or whether it's economic. And so I do mention to folks that I think we've got to step up

- whatever side you're on with these issues -you've got to step up your involvement in the political process as well as in the economic process. Whether you're for dilution, you think we should include more people in the definition of minority, then that's what you should advocate for; if you do not, we need to hear that too. So part of the confusion we've had is, that's what politicians have heard, that's what businesses have heard. It's okay, we've not complained. I think we need to change that.

Louis Green: This conversation harkens me back to the famous quote from the former NMSDC President Harriet Michel, who says Supplier Diversity is now defined as everybody except straight white men, because so many things have been added to that definition. And so I think attention needs to be paid...I'm from the perspective that we need to look at this as a national economic issue in terms of everything that affects our tax base, our military security. How well minority businesses do is not an issue of doing something for people of color, but it's going to be how go minority businesses, so will the country go. And anything else that dilutes from that, I take exception to it, because I want my grandkids not to have to eat cat food. I don't want to eat cat food myself and that's probably my future, but I don't want it for them. So that's number one. Number two, corporations, in their economic interests and self-interests, and that's what they should do, that's why I own stock, I want them to do well. Reggie lays out some ways they look at it, and JCI is exceptional; but as those pools grow, obviously the focus and the quote/unquote "pie" doesn't grow, and so that's the problem. It's not the definition, but resources matched to that, as you articulated. But that definition takes away where our field of focus should be.

Scott Vowels: One of the common themes I've heard from everyone on the panel is, we go back to the economics of it. I worked for General Motors in Purchasing, and we had sales quotas, we had profit targets, we had goals, set cost-saving goals. Whyare those words forbidden when we talk about anything having to do with minority business development, minority supplier development, or Supplier Diversity? We can't talk about quotas, targets, goals - and if every other facet of how a corporation is measured successfully uses those words, why are they so off-limits when we talk about this if it's truly an economic initiative?

Louis Green: You answered your own question. It's not an economic initiative. Those companies that measure it the same way they measure quality, profit and loss, it's more of an economic issue for them. For others who don't, it's not. It's couched to many in the C-suite as a zero-sum game. If this woman or this minority gets a contract, it's going to take away from this white male's contract, and that shouldn't be the viewpoint. I think that's part of the problem, because people see if someone gains, I'm going to lose - and the majority of the people in the C-suite are still that straight white male. You have that dynamic, so people are uncomfortable saying I want to measure how we engage our number of diverse suppliers, or how much value they're adding. Reggie, you're an exception, but you could probably speak to it better.

Reginald Layton: I want to shift the context. Johnson Controls is very successful in working with diverse suppliers. We are going to end up at $1.8 billion this year. But it's not about goals, targets, quotas - it's actually about projects and dollars. First of all, what generates the need to have a supplier? A project. It's not about a pie where we're doling out dollars and oh I'm done with my dollar pie. It's about we need to have a specific task done, who can do it, are they diverse, will it help us satisfy our customers if we have a diverse supplier? It's a different framework to look at it. And then, on top of that, are there incumbents with poor performance who refuse to do business JCI's way, who want to give us a cost increase? Why would we stay with an incumbent because of momentum and inertia, when you have a whole vast pool of excellent minority- and women-owned companies? We don't look at it as 'we have to have a goal for this'—we've got to have diverse suppliers who can do these projects to solve our incumbent problem, or to solve our not exceeding customer expectation problem. So for us, we use the language 'goals,' 'targets' because we're trying to accomplish something else, solve a problem, and minority suppliers and women-owned companies are a portfolio of folks who can help us do that. So it's a different way of looking at it, I think.

Richard Huebner: Scott, I wouldn't categorically say that corporations don't use those metrics. My experience is the corporations that are really driving progress in minority business development are very metrics-focused. They have goals, strong goals, they are articulated throughout the organization, people are held accountable to it, and they can track their return on investment. Where we're failing in some organizations and we're losing ground in Supplier Diversity is where the Supplier Diversity professional can't justify their existence on the basis of metrics. The higher I go in a corporation, the more the talk is in numbers. So we have to be able to relate to the pressing priorities, and those are largely metrics; and so we have to be able to justify our existence by documenting our successes as relates to the corporate goals. And there are plenty of companies here today that I could point to and say are very strong champions, very effective, where Supplier Diversity is becoming part of their culture because they are being driven by metrics.

Scott Vowels: I'd like to hear from the government side.

Donald Cravins: I'm sitting here and I've been listening. Dick, you said something at the onset that I've been trying to stop thinking about. I have been waiting a long time to hear a white guy say that black business economics is what is going to make the black community successful. And I know you guys are talking about corporate stuff and I don't want to get you off of that, but let me tell you why that's important. I live in Washington, but I'm a Louisiana boy and I read the Times-Picayune every day - and Perry, I read the Advocate every day. I'm 40 years old, and since the time I was 19, I've seen African American boys kill each other every day. In this city of New Orleans, we have as bad of an epidemic as we've ever had; in the city of Baton Rouge, we've got probably the worst epidemic we've ever had. And I am now convinced as a former politician, as someone who used to run for office and thought 'I could save the day,' I am now convinced that the only way we can really raise ourselves out of this is through economics. We've always said that. But Dick, I am now convinced that the only way we can make our communities better is to have thriving African American businesses in those communities hiring people, creating jobs and creating good family models. And so as we have this great discussion about black businesses and what we should be doing and whether we need diversity or not, I just hope we really, as we leave here and all of you watching in the audience understand, and our brothers and sisters who may be white or from another community, understand that's really what it's all about. We should be tired of incarcerating people and paying that bill. We should be tired of the amount of money crime costs us. We should be tired of the amount of money terrible education costs us. And all of that will be fixed, the educational system will be fixed, with economics in the African American community. So I have had a hard time getting over that, Dick, and I appreciate you saying that this morning, because that's what this is all about.

Scott Vowels: To piggyback off of that... NMSDC started out of the '68 Chicago riots, and we've had the same definitions of what a minority business, what a minority supplier is. With the changing demographics, is it time to revisit that or does it still hold water? Marquis, let's start with you. I work for NMSDC, but unfortunately I am the moderator, so I have no opinion.

Marquis Miller: In my role at NMSDC, I work for all of you - with the exception of the federal government - because we're very clear that we are a corporate membership organization that services our corporate members and supports our MBEs as constituents. I think if I'm understanding your question, what we're really talking about is whether the definition is appropriate, accurate, sufficient. As we mark our 40th anniversary, we continue to focus on our original charter to develop and to maintain opportunities for Asian, Black, Hispanic, and Native American-owned and operated businesses - to certify them as bona-fide, to develop them and help them get to scale, connect them to corporate opportunities by virtue of our membership organization, and then of course to be an advocate for minority business globally, because we are in a global society. We are focused on excellence in global supply chains. It is entirely appropriate for us to continue focusing there because, to everybody's point, there continues to be a great need in looking at how economic impact is going to benefit our entire country as a result of these businesses developing as suppliers and contributing to economies. All the statistics that come from the Department of Commerce, from the MBDA, all suggest that minority businesses tend to hire other minorities. As someone told me when I first came into my role, if you want to turn tax burdens into taxpayers, you have to give contract opportunities to minority businesses.

Reginald Layton: So Scott, I want to look at your question a little differently. The National Minority Supplier Development Council does have the important role with those demographics, but I want to focus in on the definition and what they do for

Corporate America. They certify that a company is owned, operated and controlled by a minority management team. They do the due diligence on the desk audit of the documentation and the site visit to make sure that these companies are who they say they are. That might seem like a little thing, but we had a perfect lesson in what happens when there's nobody watching the documentation and making sure people are who they say they are. We saw it in the housing market: 'Oh you look like you can afford this house, you look like this would be a good payment for you.' Whole industries went down because there was nobody doing what NMSDC does, checking the documentation, certifying that these folks can do what they say they can do and that they are who they say they are. So does NMSDC need to expand who they're doing it with? Perhaps. But so long as they stay to their core of doing the due diligence and documenting for their corporate members who owns, operates and controls these entities that look like they're historically underutilized. I think that's the key point.

Scott Vowels: One of the things I'm always hearing, and this is just in my role, is that some of my MBEs don't want to be designated as MBEs because it stigmatizes them and possibly limits their opportunities. They don't want to be designated as an MBE or a DBE because it says they are small or incapable. The term MBE or DBE is associated with inferior in some cases. Louis, what do you think about that?

Louis Green: You're right. It is associated with that. Even the language - 'give' an MBE a contract - MBEs are just as good as or usually better than anyone else, but we talk about 'giving' an MBE a contract like it's some favor. What's kind of implicit in the language we use, that perception is there. I will say in full disclosure, when I owned my business it wasn't certified. I had a white guy who I named as president who would go to all the sales meetings and would do everything, and I had lots of business for a long time. Chrysler eventually found out I was minority-owned, and said 'You need to get certified.' I've been doing business with you for four years and you never knew it. I haven't worked with the Supplier Diversity Department. If you pay for it I'll think about doing it, but why should I? Some people are scared of getting into the box. Flip side is, though, there are some great companies, especially some Fortune 1000 companies that are really committed to help because it is part of their mission, help them to grow. Being candid, I think you need to look at the sector that you're in. In some sectors, it's probably fine; in other sectors, you honestly need to think about having a front person out there to do that. It's unfortunate that's where we are, but businesses look at that right now.

Scott Vowels: You didn't hear it from Louis, but have a front-person out there. I'm just taking notes. And don't worry that this is on YouTube.

Louis Green: No, I'm not worried about it at all.

Scott Vowels: Go ahead, Don.

Donald Cravins: I think it's important that those folks who don't want that designation don't get the designation. For those folks who do want the designation, it's important for groups like this to continue the education. I don't look at it as give a DBE business, I look at it as award a qualified DBE through a competitive process, a contract. We get certified - it doesn't say once you're certified, you're guaranteed business. You getting certified in the 8A program of the SBA Small Business Administration doesn't mean you get a contract - it's not a contracting program according to the SBA, it's an economic development program. And so

DBEs and all the other acronyms still have an obligation to be a good businessman or a good businesswoman.

Louis Green: But Don, the problem is this: When there's a mishap you'll hear 'Dammit, we used an MBE and they screwed up. I'll never use an MBE again.' I've never heard 'I'll never use a white company again.' But you will hear repeatedly, 'This minority business messed up on this. We'll never use an MBE again.' Some businesses have to shoulder the burden of everyone.

Donald Cravins: But you and I have been shouldering burdens for a long time, and we continue shouldering burdens every time I see somebody on TV who looks like me who does something stupid, that I don't have to walk out of the house and they think I'm that guy too. That's just part of our obligation and our burden. So I'm with you. That's where good DBEs do have an extra obligation to do a great job, so even when brothers and sisters don't do a great job you've also pulled them up too. That's just part of life. I don't think you throw the baby out with the bathwater. I don't think you let a company who's done business with a DBE say 'Man we had a bad opportunity, let's just get rid of our DBE program.' We can't do that because the vast majority of DBEs are great and they go out there every day, they work hard and get a contract because they have a great business.

Louis Green: But even the language: 'disadvantaged business.'

Donald Cravins: But they are.

Louis Green: They're not disadvantaged. They're economically screwed over, but they aren't disadvantaged. They're more capable than more than half of the people out here. So my problem again is with the language.

Donald Cravins: I understand. I'm with you.

Scott Vowels: Dick, you've been doing this for 25 years. What's your perspective?

Richard Huebner: Word on the street in Houston is that you'll know a company is certified by the Houston Minority Supplier Development Council because the last words out of their mouth, not the first, is that they're a minority business enterprise. If we're doing our job, we're empowering them with the information and insight to be able to go in and talk at a competent level. But I think it also begs roles. What does certification mean? Does it mean you're just a minority business - minority owned, managed and controlled? Or does it mean that you're really in a position to be able to do business with major companies, that you've been through some training, some vetting if you will? Do we have the data? So our role as an organization, I think, changes from just going out and identifying them to really preparing them to be successful in this market, and that's challenging. It also says that we could be collaborative, we can work with a whole lot of organizations that share our mission - maybe at different levels with a different focus - and I think the key to that is let's not try to do all things to all people. Let's get focused on the problem, divvy up responsibilities, and let's get the problem resolved. Our Board has recently said that the Council has become very effective in positioning minority firms so they can effectively compete for, win, and perform on contracts with major corporations. They said 'But we aren't satisfied.' We want the Council to position minority firms in such a manner that business is attracted to them because they're that good, and because you said so. Changing role. So we listen to our customers and say, 'How do we take it to the next level?' We have a whole lot of organizations that are competing with us, they see what success we've had and they say 'I want to do it too, I want to cash in on this.' And my feeling is, we don't need to compete. You do it. Now that you know how to do that, let us raise our level of support and leadership to another level that we're now prepared to do, that they're not quite prepared to do yet. So go ahead, there's plenty of work for all of us to do in Supplier Diversity. Let's divvy up the responsibilities and get the job done.

Scott Vowels: Reggie, you look like you're about to explode if I don't let you comment.

Reginald Layton: I think about the question that you're asking, and I hear it a lot from diverse suppliers, 'Why do you have to have me in this classification?'. And my response is, if you're a diverse supplier you can't have it both ways. On the one hand, you want me to be able to answer the question, 'Well how much do you do with diverse businesses? Where are they located? How have you helped communities of color and women grow?'. You want me to be able to answer those questions, but you don't want me to be able to see who those people are. You want me to be not credible. Do you understand, as we said previously on the panel, that the higher you go up in an organization the more metric-driven it is, so you want me to not have a metric on our performance with diverse suppliers and the impact and out-comes we've had. Is that what you want? 'Well it just costs me money, I don't want to do it.' Okay, do you want me to promote your business throughout Johnson Controls? Do you want me to promote somebody who looks like they're diverse and we all dis-cover, like the Cincinnati public school example, that the folks they thought were diverse suppliers weren't. You can't have it both ways. If you're afraid to be stigmatized by this designation, then don't sign up for it. You can play your cards the way you see best. But if you want us to help you grow your business, it comes with the territory. That's what I want to say.

Marquis Miller: In the interest of maintaining our focus on precise language, what I meant by 'give opportunity' is really to give chances to those firms that have demonstrated their capabilities and capacity - not give them contracts for the sake of just giving them because it's not something that they're owed. It's something they work at, and the certification process validates that they've worked at it such that they can now participate in the supply chain.

Donald Cravins: Maybe we're talking about two different types of minority businesses too. You make a good point. If a brother or sister has a successful business, why should they be lumped in as a socially disadvantaged business for a certain program? I don't think we should get rid of the disadvantaged business, because they are people of color who are still very much disadvantaged and deserve a play in that role. But maybe there needs to be the creation of a new program. I've been trying to float this idea, particularly among African American, Hispanic and some other minority communities - we've got a lot of successful minority-owned businesses in this room - and I'm speaking from the government standpoint, that if you mentor or do business with an SDB, you may no longer be socially disadvantaged. You may have graduated out of the 8A program because you're successful now; you're not socially disadvantaged anymore. Why couldn't we create a program where there would be some incentive for you now to mentor the socially disadvantaged? You're no longer an SDB, you may be just a minority business owner, but maybe we shouldn't lump people into just one fit classification because it worked when we created the program in the 1960s or 1970s. I don't think we get rid of the original intent, because we still have the same problems and maybe we need to expand opportunity for small businesses.

Reginald Layton: So we're being precise in our terms. This is one of the major differences between the public sector and the private sector. The political sector, of course, has political undertones; in the private sector, you can have a huge minority business and, to Louis's point, there still might be the stigma associated with them being a minority business enterprise. I mean, World Wide Technology, they're $4 billion dollars.

Louis Green: We have billion dollar companies that have the stigma.

Reginald Layton: Yeah. Bridgewater Interiors, Software House International…these are all billion dollar companies with thousands and thousands of employees and they're not small, they're not disadvantaged, but they are minority. So, we need to be precise in our terms, design our programs accordingly and yes, we can have those programs, particularly in the private sector where they're designed to address a specific issue: diversify the supply chain, go after market opportunities or whatever.

Scott Vowels: I think it's clear that we all realize how important Supplier Diversity and minority business programs are, both in the corporate arena and the government arena. Maybe it's just me, but why is it that I'm seeing more corporations cut back on their Supplier Diversity programs in terms of funding, why I'm getting more resumes from former Supplier Diversity program managers? And I can't let the government slide, because I got a note six or seven months ago that they were closing all the local MBDA offices. So if we care so much in all these arenas, why are we shutting it down if we care and it's important?

Reginald Layton: I'm the corporation on the panel, so let me try to help. Johnson Controls - eight years ago I had nine people on my team, okay? Now we're down to four, so on the surface it looks like we're cutting the program. Johnson Controls is part of the building construction industry and the automotive industry, two industries that were severely impacted by the financial crash in 2008. And, of course, my budget is frozen. So what's the good side in all this? We applied our resources more innovatively. We leveraged technology, so our spend has doubled in the last eight years because now we don't have a person going around training our 2,500 buyers - and yes it's 2,500 in 300 cities - we use technology to do that. We leverage the tools of electronic profiles, rather than me taking a diverse supplier in the room with the buyer. These people are in teams in different cities; we electronically broadcast the profiles to the same people. So innovation, process improvement also have a play in this, where you see corporations reducing their staffs and you see better-qualified Supplier Diversity people. They're at a higher level; they're talking about mergers, acquisitions, joint ventures, buying divested plants. Six-hundred million of our spend came from where several MBEs bought Johnson Controls' plant, so there's a reason why there are lower staffs - but there's also good news in that we're leveraging the available resources that we have.

Louis Green: I think a couple things. I think one, we - I include myself in this - as folks who support Supplier Diversity professionals, we've done a miserable job giving them the tools they need to make a business case about the importance of their work. There are some people who get it on their own, there are some people who are fortunate to have an ecosystem of leadership where it happens; but we've done a terrible job - and maybe Dick and Marcus and you haven't, just me - I've done a terrible job of giving the tools to my corporate Supplier Diversity people so they can go in on their performance, and show how they're adding value to the company, how they can maintain some kind of close-to-C-suite relationship, which is difficult to do. We always say in best practices 'oh go march up to the CEO'. Not too many people in a Fortune 100 company go knock on the door to the CEO.

I'm just keeping it real. But we haven't given the tools to show the value. The value has always been about meeting a target... so problem is you make your eight percent target—well hell, we don't need you anymore, you won your Corporation of the Year award, we don't need you anymore. It needs to be more about a different type of value and measure it. I don't think we've done a good job giving the tools to people and helping to make that happen, and so you see programs getting cut back because they can't demonstrate the value. The one thing that made me feel good when I was at General Electric, Jeff Immelt said - because I was fortunate enough to make my case to him repeatedly - he said, 'If I have to fire 90 percent of the people in this company, you'd be one of the 10 percent of people I'd keep, because I get what you do and I understand the value to this company. And I don't think we've given the tools for people to do that on a consistent basis. And in corporate, if you can't measure it you're gone.

Richard Huebner: I think relevance and priority. I've been told by some corporate CEOs, I said, 'How come you're assigning the same value to Supplier Diversity that you assign to other programs?' and they said 'Well you're not relevant.' Oh, tell me more about that. You don't relate to the four or five things I'm interested in. I use local content as an example for companies that trade internationally, do business internationally. They are faced with requirements to use local-based firms. There's a strong emphasis on how we're going to do that. Most of those firms aren't capable of working at the level that our suppliers that we've grown over the years are capable of working at. So how do we meet those requirements? And I simply asked our chief procurement officers, "How does Supplier Diversity get the same level of commitment that you're now playing on local content?" ...and they said the difference is local content is an imperative: either you do it or you don't do business. Supplier Diversity is still a possibility, a preference, possibly something that we're interested in if we get around to it - but we don't have to do it. Somewhere, we need to assign higher priority. The companies that have assigned high priority to minority business development are the ones who are performing at that level. Getting to the CEO, the cost-cutting that Reggie's talking about, that's common; doing more with less, that's common. Let's not disguise that for the fact that we still have to show through metrics, I believe, our return on investment in Supplier Diversity proves that value, and raises the priority within the company to a level comparable to efforts like local content.

Donald Cravins: You mentioned the Minority Business Development Agency, which is run by the Department of Commerce. How many in the audience, just by a show of hands, are familiar with the Minority Business Development Agency? Okay, keep your hands up. How many of you heard that there may be cuts to the Minority Business Development Agency? Alright, so the people who are watching online, I don't think they can see this but we've a couple of hands up. Of those of you with your hands up, how many of you, when you heard that, emailed your congressman or congresswoman or your United States senator, or the president? Okay, two or three, four. That's what it's all about in the public sector; that's what it's about in the public sector. When we hear these things ladies and gentlemen, I think, you know, for a while we kind of got accustomed to either bad things happening and there's not much we can do to change it - or maybe, with this administration, bad things can't happen. And that's not the political reality or the public reality, sometimes, of government: decisions aren't always made - I'm trying to keep my job up here - that way. You've got to be an advocate; you've got to be an advocate. So when you hear about those decisions, that the Department of Commerce is considering something, you've got to be an advocate. And it's so easy these days to be an advocate.

Louis Green: Email.

Donald Cravins: You can shoot an email very quickly. Other groups do it. I'm here to tell you other groups do that. They are advocates for what they believe in. So when we talk about the definitions have expanded, there's a reason for that, because some group advocated 'we want to be in this definition, we want to participate in this program, we want the benefits.' Advocate.

Scott Vowels: Not that everybody on this panel would have an idea, but why does it seem like there is such apathy among the minority supplier community? If other groups are willing to come up, knock on the door whether it's corporations or the government, why do you think there's—unless I'm clueless, I've never heard of a minority supplier think tank, a minority business think tank. NMSDC is the closest thing we've got. Why do you think there's a sense of apathy - or I find a sense of apathy or something? Something's amiss among our minority suppliers.

Marquis Miller: I'll say that I don't know that it's apathy. I think in what's been said on the panel so far, it is really about business owners being in business, keeping their head down, focusing on building their competencies and delivering their products on time, on budget - not that they're not interested in being more visible, more vocal as advocates, but they're really focused on building and strengthening their business. I think that the difference between the public sector and the private sector is primarily the fact that the government is working on a public interest platform, and the private sector is working in its own enlightened self-interest. And I don't mean that as a pejorative, it's just the way business gets done; and where there are businesses that are committed, they have tended to be committed on two levels: one because it's in their enlightened self-interest from a community standpoint - their employees, their community face, if you will - and then ultimately, to Reggie's point, their need for more innovation in an increasingly competitive environment. But then I also would say that they, in doing business with the government based on the government's public interest platform, want to comply with the government's interest in ensuring that there is opportunity for the public. We look at it that way. I don't think that it's apathy as much as people just, again, being really focused and now that there is more of an issue at hand, there may be more of an interest and willingness to be more publicly involved. But I don't know that I would call it apathy.

Donald Cravins: And as I meet with folks - African American business owners, Hispanic business owners across the U.S. - I don't sense apathy. I sense that these are men and women who are working very hard, keeping their head down trying to get it done. I think the difference between our minority business groups and some of the other groups is they've got one message, a paid advocacy group…

Louis Green: There it is.

Donald Cravins: …who goes to the Hill on their behalf, and it's a clear message. I hear a lot of little messages here. In New Orleans, I hear from great businessmen and women who give me a great message and I try to take it back; and then I'm in Dallas and I hear - you guys have a fantastic organization in Dallas, Texas - I hear great messages from them. On the Hill, very seldom is there one message, and it's a message that 'Oh that so-and-so, he or she advocates for minority business interest, he or she advocates for the 8A program, he or she advocates, and every time I see that person I know they're there working on those interests.' We don't have that, by and large. We don't have that in our community. Other groups do, they do. You know who the lobbyist is for this organization or that organization, you know what their job is. Their job is to make sure they're watching to make sure that the programs aren't cut, they're watching to make sure those centers aren't cut, and they're also there to advocate to do some new things, to strengthen programs. We don't have that one voice on Capitol Hill, and that's not to offend anybody. There's some, but it's not the same. It's not the same. The message is not always being delivered concisely.

Richard Huebner: I would say it's not really apathy - it's more skepticism. 'My vote doesn't count, nobody really is going to do anything anyway, Supplier Diversity doesn't work'—there are plenty of examples that would support that. So 80 percent of small businesses don't make it five years. There are a lot of people out there who are not making it, and we don't do a really good job of positioning those who do. There's also a different attitude, I would say, in minority communities, where if you've been born and raised in America and you hear about this as a land of opportunity, your life experience has not necessarily been supportive of that. But if you come in from another country today and you come to America thinking that this is the land of opportunity, chances are you're going to succeed a lot faster than perhaps even the white people born in this country who are conditioned with that skepticism—'I've tried it, I've seen other people try it and it doesn't work.' But a lot of the immigrants are coming in to this country and doing exceptionally well, because they come here with little resources but a great attitude. I think part of that is really providing a broader depth of support to the firms - but also get into, as Marquis said, their headset to help adjust the headset and help them understand that, wait a minute, this is the land of opportunity. Let's pursue it as if it was.

Louis Green: Dick, I agree with you, but Don makes a point. If you take the 15,000 larger businesses just in the NMSDC network— MBEs, minority businesses—if each of them said 'I'm going to put $100 towards a lobbying firm to advocate for… So with a billion and a half dollars, you could have a lobbyist in D.C., a good lobbying firm to keep your interests in front of everybody.

Scott Vowels: I'd do that.

Louis Green: That would make all the difference. There is no voice there in D.C., there's no consistent voice or message on the Hill, and it doesn't cost that much to get a good credible lobbying firm who's committed to doing that to keep that message in front of everybody. And I don't want to sound like one of the late night—'for only 30 cents a day you can sponsor a child'—but for only a couple pennies a day, you can have your business in front, top of mind. But MBEs are going to have to own that and make that happen.

Donald Cravins: And who's doing it on a state level? We're talking about Washington D.C., there are a lot of state policies that affect businesses as well. Who does it on a local level? Who lobbies at the city council of New Orleans for African American businesses? And there may be someone, I'm just saying you've got to look at it at all those levels. Other people do, other groups do. That's in the public sector and, again, I'm not the business guy up here but I'm the government guy up here. Ladies and gentlemen, that's how it works. Your elected representatives who you've put in office, they've got to hear from you, they've got to know what's important to you, they've got to know what issues matter to you, and that's how our democracy works - and we have an obligation as African American, Hispanic, minority business owners, white business owners - you do have an obligation to make sure that your voice is heard to your elected representatives. Some of you do, but is that voice concise, is that voice loud and clear? It's not enough just to have black elected officials on your city council or in Congress or in your state legislature. It's not enough.

Scott Vowels: I feel like we've picked on the government a little bit here, but I love and respect Don so I'm going to do my best to make sure he keeps his job. So I'm going to lay off of you for just a second.

Donald Cravins: Thank you. Momma's got to eat.

Scott Vowels: One of the trends I find - and again it may just be me - one of the trends that I find disarming within the corporate Supplier Diversity programs is that percentages of spend will get reported; and then when we do a little bit bigger, better digging, we find out that certain services or products may be left out of the overall, so we're not taking the percentage from the overall spend. And Reggie, I'm going to leave you for last on this one.

Reginald Layton: Okay.

Scott Vowels: Marquis, Dick, Louis - do you find that? What do you think about it? Is it happening or is it just some corporations? Not in Northern California, I need to keep my job, Don.

Louis Green: Yeah, of course corporations do it. Some do, not all. Some people will say they have business reasons, some people are trying to meet a number for whatever reasons - for contracts, for public face, whatever. Others are more serious about their numbers and the integrity of their numbers, and most companies don't treat their minority Supplier Diversity numbers with the same integrity as they will with other numbers. It can be a little soft, a little loose. Reggie, you're looking at me like you might disagree. I think most companies don't keep good numbers. I doubt if most CEOs, if they had to stand behind their numbers, they wouldn't do it because most of them are soft numbers. I think the bigger issue, Scott, is really about value - because it's easy for a large corporationpotentially. You can have a shell MBE company doing everything in your system, you have a big number, but you aren't adding any value, you're not creating jobs, it's not getting down to communities. It really should be the impact of the spend as opposed to the spend itself. The spend only means so much. If I told you, and I come from a place where we've got lots of companies who do over billions of dollars a year, but it's really about the impact of that spend - and I think we've always been focused on the number and the percentage and we should measure the impact, the lives transformed, the jobs created in communities. Those numbers, there are some more meaningful numbers.

Donald Cravins: And who measures the numbers?

Louis Green: They measure their own numbers.

Scott Vowels: Companies do.

Donald Cravins: Who compiles the numbers? You made a great point earlier - you talked about a think tank. Where is that African American think tank in this country? I ask this question all the time. There are a couple of organizations that have economists. I know the National Urban League has a fantastic economist, and I was with her at the last convention, Dr. Wilson. But I ask this question all the time: Where in America is there a group of men and women whose sole purpose is to measure those things, whether it be in the private sector? We want to see what impact the minority programs are having. We want to measure the public sector, and now, we will have a message. So when we do hire our lobbyist - to my right - we will have a message, because we've got good numbers. I ask this question all the time: Where are the numbers? Who is our think tank? Where is our think tank? Other groups have think tanks, plenty of think tanks on the other side, right? Where are our numbers?

Louis Green: And that would open the platform for MBEs. This is the tax revenue we're putting into your community, this is what we're creating in your district. When you do that, it empowers you, it empowers the MBEs to do lots of stuff, and helps you make a stronger case. It helps Reggie in his job, right?

Richard Huebner: So I can say from a local level, 20 years into this field, I have never used the numbers that the corporation has reported to me…because they weren't comparable. I couldn't compare them against each other. They weren't credible, frankly. They were reporting people that they thought were minority businesses. We, about six years ago, went to an effort where we now send them the list of firms and say 'Write in the column next to the list the amount you spent with that firm.' If they're not on the list, they don't count. Now I can do that at the local level, but then that gives me a wealth of information because I can marry that up to the database, and I can find out what fields are we excelling in, what are we over-crowded in, where are the opportunity areas for minority business that we need to begin moving people to? I think, to the credit of a lot of our corporations in Houston, particularly in the oil and gas industry, where they've said: 'okay most of our spend is in downstream, most of our spend with minority firms is in downstream, but there's a huge opportunity in upstream, but we don't have many minority firms.' So a concerted effort to try to move some firms who have achieved excellence in downstream operations to the upstream, where there's more money and more opportunity. Having that metrics, locally, that justifies our existence – but, more importantly, empowers us to one: recognize companies who are really doing it, and two: be credible as the authority of minority business development, and three: flesh out the opportunities. What's the reality and what's the opportunity?

Scott Vowels: Go ahead.

Marquis Miller: In the context of this panel, subtitled *'The Future of Supplier Diversity'*, it's really having more diversity in thought and application of the processes that really make up the end-game, which is to take, as Dick mentions, those firms that have this successful downstream and develop them so they can do business upstream. That's essentially the essence of our 40 years of focusing on supplier development. There are organizations that do business development - some of those organizations operate with the think tank mindset. There are chambers that are focused on advocating for those businesses, but it's probably safe to say that every business is not a supplier. So the focus on how you now develop those suppliers is really how you start to drive the metrics, because that's what the companies are paying attention to. How are these collections of businesses going to help us with our corporate goals and objectives?

Scott Vowels: Uh oh. Corporate man, sorry.

Reginald Layton: So Scott, you asked a question about what we call in the Supplier Diversity world 'excludables.' What do you take out of the calculation so that your numbers look better? In Johnson Controls' case, our program, our initiative, our efforts, our processes are only 16 years old. So in my book, we're novices at this, we're young in doing this. So there are a lot of bad habits that we never picked up - we didn't know that people excluded things. I didn't find that out until I was in the job for eight years. I was like, 'You exclude capital equipment? Really? Why would you do that?'. So we don't exclude anything but salaries, taxes, and contributions. Everything else is fair game. Now, what I hear from my colleagues is, 'Well, there are industries where there are no minorities' - and I say 'How do you know that? How do you know that?' And then they say 'Well there are no aluminum smelters', and I say 'Well you know what, we had that situation in our battery group, there were no lead smelters, we thought, until we checked.' Every day, minority companies and minority management teams are buying existing companies or forming companies. You can't say let's exclude something in the calculation because you believe that they aren't there. It's our job as Supplier Diversity professionals to check. The other thing that's the answer to this is you don't exclude things if you're buying it from a company that's part of the calculation. Then it's all about integrity. We don't do this calculation on percentages - our projects are denominated in dollars. How much is this project worth? A million dollars, not 10 percent - what is that? So there's a whole orientation on the calculation: projects are denominated in dollars, work is denominated in dollars, the metrics are denominated in dollars, the goals are in dollars, everything's in dollars. Since we are going to have numbers-based metrics, let's deal with that. I was looking at the numbers: you heard me say that we're going to end the fiscal year 2012 at $1.8 billion. Okay, so that's 565 minority and women-owned companies, 80 percent of those are minority-owned companies that are certified. We've got another 300 that are alleged, that don't count. I looked at the number of employees they have: 93,000 employees. That's 93,000 jobs. So your point about having an advocacy mechanism in the public sector is important, because you would provide that type of data: 93,000 jobs are depending on these 560 diverse companies doing services for just Johnson Controls. The other thing: How do you get this type of information? The councils, NMSDC, they have to push the idea of surveillance systems. You cannot run a program managing 560 plus diverse companies on a spreadsheet. And I didn't mention that there are another 1,100 in the queue, with 2,500 buyers all over the country - and that's not counting the ones not sitting in the United States. You cannot do it without surveillance systems where you could pick up this data, and have an intelligent conversation with your management and the public sector. The other thing: cascading the requirements to other corporations. In our world, we call this 'second tier.' Yeah, you could give them a percentage, but you could say 'No, I want a solution from you. I want a solution from you, Mr. Prime, that involves women and minority-owned companies'. Eighty-eight of JCI's primes rose to the occasion. When I looked at their numbers, they only spent $111 million. That's not much compared to our $1.8 billion. But they managed 963 minority and women-owned companies with all the jobs that that brings to the table. So my point is, when you deal with excludables - you pull on that thread - there's a lot to it. You need to have surveillance systems, you need to promote as organizations integrity around what the numbers are, killing this idea of excluding things to make the percentage look better. Don't even deal with percentages - deal with dollars and projects, and what are they?

Louis Green: Reggie, let me push back on you on one thing. Do you or others that you know usethe number I like is a POP number, a 'percentage of possibilities'? If I could have used MBEs for everything on this project, forget the dollars, right? Did I use 100 percent of available MBEs on this project? Did I use 50 percent, 10 percent? On a billion-dollar project, your POP number might only be 12 percent of MBEs. The book's available on Amazon, if you want to get my book about POPbecause that really tells me something about your effort. If there's an opportunity, and you could have used MBEs on all 100 percent of that - if your number is 100 on that project - it tells me a lot about what's going on there. Do you or do any of your Billion Dollar Roundtable folks use POP numbers?

Reginald Layton: My body language is suggesting I'm struggling with the POP number idea, and I want to tell you why: only because it's an end-of-the-game metric. I'm more concerned about the process that leads to the POP number. So, for example, at Johnson Controls we have a project pipeline and we have a top projects list. So if you notice the impact is on the process, how many projects are on the top project list? What are the ratings on those projects? Which ones are going to convert, which ones are going to be MBE, which ones are going to be WBE, what's the probability that they will pop before the end of the year, how much is the POP value? So it's not the POP number at the end. It's this process of tracking the project, filling out what the project pipeline is where you can articulate what are the requirements, where are they, how much are they, when will they happen, who are the diverse suppliers? That's what I want the conversation to be about.

Louis Green: No, I understand the conversation but the metrics at the end. If you could say 'You know what, this was a $10 million project, we used every MBE possible on this project. That might have only been two percent of that project, or it could have been 82 percent of that project. But if the MBEs who were in that pipeline were competitive and won that business, that tells you where you need to get more MBEs in that particular pipeline or along a project. The POP number basically says, did you do your very best?

Reginald Layton: Let me tell you how we would interpret the POP number. The POP number is: did we get all the projects that are available for anybody to do? How many MBEs worked on those projects, period? And, if they take the whole project, good - if they have part of the project, good - if they bring us an innovation where we add to the project pipeline, good. So it's not how many projects were totally saturated with the MBE doing all the work - it's how much participation did we have on all the projects that we have available for anybody to do? So it's a different way.

Scott Vowels: I know the conversation's getting good when people start using those imaginary quotes, because I saw you do that with POP.

Louis Green: It's not imaginary.

Scott Vowels: One of the other things. This is a time when I wish I would have paid more attention in second or third grade doing math, because I was at the $1.8 billion trying to divide it by 565 suppliers and figure out about how much that is per supplier, but I couldn't. I had a $2 billion supplier out of a $1.8 billion spend - I don't know what happened. So anyway, coming back full circle with the government and with corporations, the thing I'm hearing about is capacity - they've got to have capacity. Government, MBDA, and I apologize for not knowing these statistics offhand, but either they want to deal with $500,000 businesses or million-dollar businesses. Within the corporations, the supply chains have gotten so global, so they need businesses that have capacity. And I look at my database of over 800 suppliers and 37 percent of them are a million dollars or less in revenue. So I'm going to leave the majority of my suppliers - and that average revenue of that 37 percent is $238,000, so mine cannot play according to the rules by MBDA and corporations if we're saying they have to be certain capacity sizes.

Reginald Layton: That's a myth. I have to say it—it's a myth that all diverse suppliers have to be large. That is not how it's done. The requirements of a project are based on what's needed. Some projects, you need a global supplier with large capital and big employee bases; other projects you don't. I'm going to give you an example: If you're building a car, yeah, you need to have a supplier of some capacity. If you're wiring a building, electrical contractor, they don't need to be one thousand employees. Videographers, they can be sole proprietors. Advertising firms.

So the myth is an easy answer: 'Oh they all need to have capacity.' The reality is the capacity that's needed is based on what needs to be done. If it's a big thing that needs to be done, you need big capacity; if it's a whole bunch of little things that need to be done, little is fine. We would not hire, you know, Stephen Spielberg to videotape a corporate meeting - I mean, come on. So the reality is, the requirements match the needs. We don't have electrical contractors from China wiring buildings in the United States - that doesn't make sense. You see what I'm saying? So it's not a pat answer of 'we need big'. It depends on what the project requirements are, and we match the supplier capabilities based on those project requirements. That's the reality.

Scott Vowels: Go ahead, Dick. Sorry.

Richard Huebner: I think it's a function of role and value. So let's talk about role. The major process has been in the past: large corporation does business with large prime supplier, who is asked to use minority businesses or the subcontracting role in construction, which generally hasn't allowed the minority firm to really grow to a significant capacity. But today, what we're seeing is minority firms bringing new solutions to the table that entitle them, because of their direct relationship and knowledge and insight of the corporate needs, they're now able to bring in the bigger partners. And it's not a front operation. It's that the minority firm has done the work, it's developed the relationship, and it understands the scope of the project better than the larger prime that they bring in to handle the capacity needs. So strategically teaming, I think, it really important. I think also value - we have a corporation present today that made a presentation to our Chief Procurement Officer Summit, and the gist of their presentation was, you know, the real opportunity for minority business is to help that corporation bring them new business.

Reginald Layton: Right.

Richard Huebner: And so here's a corporation that has very strong ties throughout Houston, very well politically connected. But I was looking into growing into another area of the country where they don't have those political ties, nor do they have the capability to do what they need to do or want to do there. They do the bankroll, and so they can bankroll the project - but they need some people on the ground that have the technical expertise to get it done and the political connections to get them awarded the opportunity to do that. And so, where do they turn? They turn to minority businesses, and those minority businesses in that particular part of the country are able to open up a whole scope of new business for this corporation. And so the idea of - and the point was made at the Chief Procurement Officer Summit - that the idea of just replacing one supplier with another supplier just isn't going to get us anywhere. They've already been through that, they've already eliminated, they've become married to a lot of the suppliers they do have. We're going to have to look for role and value.

Donald Cravins: You talked about the Minority Business Development Agency creatinga program for small businesses, minority small businesses with capacity. And I've talked to Director Hinson about this at length, and I think he's got it right. What his opinion and President Obama's opinion is, the Small Business Administration has programs designed for small, small businesses- microbusinesses - that's when we talk about the 8A program. It is for socially disadvantaged and economically disadvantaged small businesses. When that small businessman or woman builds capacity, they're kicked out of the program because it's an economic development program. What Director Hinson is thinking is there has to be a continuum for the next level of African American-owned small businesses, and there's absolutely nothing wrong with that. That goes back to our original point. Maybe we need to look at programs that take small business from the beginning and, as they want to grow - rather than kicking them out and saying 'Alright, you're good. Fall off that cliff. You're not going to get any more government contracts, you should have capacity by now' -create other programs. One thing that my boss has wanted to do - and I'd love some advocacy from some of you if you think that it's something we should - in America, we define small business as 500 or less, and then you're other than small. We have no mid-tier businesses in America. And so what happens to a lot of minority businesses is, as they grow and build capacity through some of these great programs for the small businesses of America, they fall off the cliff - or they intentionally stay small so they don't get pushed off the cliff, which doesn't create jobs in the African American community. What if we created a mid-tier size business, people who graduate from the small business program, and for those businesses we created some preference programs for them? If you mentor a small business, you mentor a socially disadvantaged business - we're going to give you a couple extra points so you can now compete. You're still competing against the Boeings and the Lockheeds right now - we want to change that. We want to give you some level playing field with some of the big companies. I would love to see the creation of that program in America, where we would look at businesses as small, medium, and large. I'd need your help to do that. I'd need your help to do that, if you agree. If you don't, tell me you don't and we won't do it. But I think where Director Hinson was going with the MBDA was, we've got programs for really small businesses - let's try to do something for the next level African American-owned small business, because they need some help too.

Scott Vowels: Okay. So I've learned a couple of very valuable things up here this evening - or this morning. One is that when

174 | Scott A. Vowels PhD

you're going to be on YouTube on stage, you really need to wear socks that have more elastic, because mine keep falling down around my ankles and that could be very embarrassing on YouTube. The second is that when we decide to open it up to Twitter and some other things, people actually care - and so you've seen me checking the phone and the questions are getting a little bit overwhelming for our Twitter group to keep forwarding to me so...

References

Adeli, J. (2012, January 23). Women-owned Small Business Opportunities in Federal Contracting. *The Solopreneur Life - Resources for Building Your Purpose-driven Solo Business.* Retrieved from http://www.thesolopreneurlife.com/women-owned-small-business-opportunities-in-federal-contracting/

DiMisa, J. (2013, March). Designing Effective Sales Quotas in Today's Market Requires Custom Tailoring. *21*(1), Retrieved from http://www.sibson.com/publications/perspectives/volume_21_issue_1/custom-tailoring.html

Doctorow, C. (2013, November 08). Rich America Versus Poor America:Stats about the Wealth Gap. Retrieved from http://boingboing.net/2013/11/08/rich-america-versus-poor-ameri.html

Greenhalgh, L., & Lowry, J. (2011). Minority Business Success: Focusing on the American Dream. Stanford, California: Stanford University Press.

Gravely, M. (2014). *The Capacity to Succeed.* (1st ed.). Cincinnati: Impact Group Publishers.

Shear, W. (2012). United States Government Accountability Office: *Government Contracting – Federal Efforts to Assist Small Minority-owned Businesses* (GAO-12-873). Retrieved from website: http://www.gao.gov/assets/650/648985.pdf

Whitfield, G. (2008). Supplier Diversity and Competitive Advantage: New Opportunities in Emerging Domestic Markets. *Graziadio Business Review, 11*(3), Retrieved from http://gbr.pepperdine.edu/2010/08/supplier-diversity-and-competitive-advantage-new-opportunities-in-emerging-domestic-markets/

Author Biography

Scott A. Vowels, PhD, is a recognized thought leader and expert in the field of Supplier Diversity. He is currently the Supplier Diversity lead for a Fortune 100 technology company and is widely known within the network for successfully leading both the Northern California and Alabama Minority Supplier Development Councils to national prominence as President and CEO. Vowels also operated an Opportunity Center for the US Department of Commerce Minority Business Development Agency. His early career involved managing procurement and sourcing processes for manufacturing environments within General Motors. His experience comprises over twenty years in procurement and supplier diversity.

Vowels is a frequent speaker and panelist on minority business issues and the co-founder and moderator for the first *The BIGGER Discussion: Future of Supplier Diversity* industry panel. He holds a doctorate and master's degree in business administration, a master's degree in economics, and is APP and CPM certified through the Institute for Supply Management.

Made in the USA
Middletown, DE
15 May 2015